Fire Flood & Failure: Real Lessons in Commercial Property Insurance

By Paul J. McCarrison

First Edition – June 2025

ISBN: 978-1-7641501-0-1

AF885615

Typeset & Prepared by: Risk Advisor Academy

This book is a work of nonfiction. All examples, cases, and claims have been adapted or fictionalised for educational purposes. While every effort has been made to ensure accuracy, the author and publisher do not offer legal, financial, or insurance advice. Readers are encouraged to consult qualified professionals for guidance related to their own circumstances.

For rights and permissions: paul@riskadvisoracademy.com

To my father, a true stalwart of the insurance profession, who put me on the path with stories and spectacles from London to New Zealand.

And to my son, the next generation - the reason I rise each day, and the heart of every dream I hold.

Contents

Preface

This book is for the broker still learning the terrain, the one who has seen enough to know what can go wrong, but not yet enough to stop it in time. Each chapter is a true or composite story, refined into a teaching moment, shared not to shame, but to sharpen.

I've seen what happens when we get it right. And what happens when we don't. The stories in this book are drawn from two decades of navigating claim calls, client panic, insurer wrangling, and the subtle art of risk placement.

Some of the lessons I learned the hard way. Others were handed to me by wiser colleagues who knew how to listen. I've included both.

I hope what follows keeps you from repeating preventable mistakes. I hope it lifts your confidence. And most of all, I hope it reminds you that what we do matters, quietly, but powerfully, to people trying to hold on to their livelihoods.

Start Here: Your Role, Your Impact

Before we dive into the flames, floods, and failures, you need to know one thing:

This book isn't just about claims. It's about people.

It's about what happens in the moments *before* the paperwork is found... When clients are standing in the street, wet socks, burnt tools, or a thousand-yard stare behind glass.

It's about your role, not as a salesperson, not even as a technical expert, but as the one person who may have asked the question that saved everything.

Why These Stories Matter

You won't find theoretical case studies here.
You'll find lived moments: the phone call, the lease clause, the misread limit, the misaligned policy, each a hinge point in someone's story.

And whether you work in Auckland, Atlanta, Manchester or Montreal, the lessons apply.
Because **risk doesn't care about geography**, but recovery does depend on insight.

A Note on Regional Voices

You'll notice many stories reference Australia and New Zealand. That's where I've worked most. But I've written this for **every broker, in every market**.

To help you bridge into your own practice:

- You'll see **"Global Equivalents"** throughout the book
- The Masterclass this book connects to includes tools for **AU, NZ, UK, US, and Canadian** markets
- And I've translated regional terminology wherever it matters

So don't let the accent fool you.

This isn't a regional guidebook.

It's a **global field manual** for commercial brokers who want to protect their clients at the moments that matter most.

One More Thing Before We Begin

You don't have to know everything. You don't have to be perfect.

But you do have to **stay present**, stay curious, and care enough to ask the second question.

That's what this book teaches.

And if, by the final chapter, you find yourself asking better questions, thinking more clearly, and carrying your clients' risks a little differently, then this book has done its job.

Let's begin.

How to Use This Book

This book isn't meant to be read once and shelved. It's a companion, a field guide for the quiet, critical moments in a broker's journey.

You might be new to insurance, still wrapping your head around what "ISR" means or why indemnity periods matter. Or perhaps you've been around a few renewals, survived your first claim, and sensed there's more to this role than policies and premiums. Either way, this book is for you.

Each chapter is built around a real or composite story. Some are cautionary tales. Others are examples of things done right. All are designed to sharpen your instincts and deepen your awareness of what truly matters in property and business interruption broking.

Here's how to get the most from it:

- **Start at the beginning, or don't.** Each chapter stands alone. You can dip into the one that feels most relevant today.
- **Reflect as you read.** Ask yourself: "Would I have caught that?" or "Have I checked this for my own clients?"
- **Don't skip the "What If..." or "Broker Insight" sections.** That's where the lesson crystalises.
- **Use the glossary.** It's there to support, not to test.
- **Return to it.** When you're reviewing a lease, placing a BI limit, or facing a difficult claim, come back. These stories will mean more the second time around.

And when you're ready to go deeper, to learn the technical strategies, the wording nuances, the checklists and real-world techniques behind every chapter. I've built a full Property & BI Masterclass just for that. It's launching soon.

But for now, stay curious. Stay present. Let each story remind you that your role matters. Quietly. Powerfully. And sometimes, heroically.

Chapter 1: The warehouse inferno

Before the reward, there must be labor. You plant before you harvest. You sow in tears before you reap."
- Ralph Ransom

Real-world case

In 2018, a warehouse fire in Greater Manchester destroyed five tenant-operated businesses leasing bays within a larger industrial unit. None had contents, stock, or fit-out insurance. The landlord's ISR policy covered the building structure only. Losses totalled over £2.4 million (approx. USD $3 million). Only one tenant reopened within 12 months.

George's story

George sat on a collapsed timber pallet in front of his still-smoking warehouse, the smell of burnt plastic and scorched insulation thick in the air. Steam curled from the concrete where the fire hoses had soaked everything into submission. His hands rested palm-down on his knees, as if he could keep himself anchored with pressure alone.

Twelve years. Gone. In twelve minutes.

He hadn't built Custom Fit Cabinets with investors or silent partners. Just a beat-up ute, a second-hand drill, and the kind of ambition that eats your weekends and holidays and calls it progress.

The business had grown. One van became three. A rented garage bay became a leased 1,000 sqm warehouse. He hired ten people. Installed mezzanine racking. Stored completed kitchen sets and commercial cabinetry, client jobs booked months in advance.

And then, one faulty lithium battery charger left plugged in overnight changed everything.

When George called his broker at 7:30 that morning, he was still shaking.

“There’s been a fire,” he said. “The whole place is gone.”

Daniel, his broker, arrived by 9:00 AM. Neat shirt, clipboard, trying not to stare.

“George,” he said quietly, “I’ve reviewed the policy. You’re listed as tenant, but not as an insured party on the landlord’s building cover. And there’s no contents policy for the stock or fit-out.”

“But I pay rent. And I filled in your insurance form.”

“The landlord covers the structure. You were responsible for everything inside. The lease says so. We never received it from you.”

“You didn’t ask.”

“I should’ve.”

No cover. No payout. No business interruption clause. Just ashes and a growing list of cancelled jobs.

George laid off his team within three weeks. He sold the utes and the remaining tools. By the end of the quarter, the company was closed.

Three months later, he walked into a new broker’s office with a burnt file box and a tight jaw.

“Tell me what I didn’t know last time,” he said. “Because I can’t afford to find out the hard way again.”

Mentor reflection

Assumptions are the most expensive part of an insurance placement.

George assumed the landlord's policy protected him. Daniel assumed the lease would come through. Both missed the moment to ask: "What happens if this place burns down?"

What if George had been asked for the lease up front?
What if a contents schedule had been completed, even on a back-of-envelope basis?
What if Daniel had walked the site? Or asked, "Who owns the mezzanine?"
The loss wouldn't have disappeared, but the payout might have made all the difference.

In hindsight, the lesson is clear: If you don't ask, you don't cover it.

Broker's checklist – tenant warehouse occupancy

- Review the lease: Clarify glass, signage, fit-outs, and insurance obligations.
- Assess all contents: Include WIP, plant, shelving, and third-party goods.
- Define fixed improvements: Mezzanines, lighting, wiring, are they insured?
- Valuate stock on site: Account for delivery, staging, and finished goods.
- Model BI exposure: Estimate downtime, rebuild timeframes, and revenue impact.
- File everything: Document cover discussions and lease assumptions explicitly.

Global lens

In Newark, NJ (2019) and Houston, TX (2020), tenant-operated units in leased industrial properties suffered uninsured losses after fires revealed that tenants were not scheduled on building policies and had no standalone contents cover. In both cases, losses exceeded USD $1.5 million, and coverage disputes lasted over 12 months.

CPD reflection

- Have you reviewed leases for all tenant-occupied industrial clients?
- Are contents, fit-outs, and BI exposures documented and covered?
- Do you know who owns the walls, the floors, the mezzanine? Does your client?

Chapter 2: The lease that undid the cover

"An ounce of prevention is worth a pound of cure."
- Benjamin Franklin

Real-world case

In 2020, a café in Sydney's inner west suffered over **AUD $180,000** in uninsured damage when high winds shattered a glass façade, flooding the premises. The tenant lease required the business owner to maintain all glass and frontage. The Business Pack policy had no glass extension, no flood cover, and no business interruption endorsement. The claim was denied in full. The business closed permanently within four months.

Olivia's story

It wasn't the rain that did it. Not really. It was the silence before it.

That Sunday night, the wind had turned feral... gutter-rattling, fence-toppling, bring-the-dog-inside kind of feral. Olivia watched it from the back steps of her townhouse with a cup of peppermint tea and a rising sense of unease.

She should've gone to check the café. Just to be sure. But the glass had held through storms before, and she hadn't wanted to seem obsessive. Her partner had already teased her once that week for double-checking the grinder calibration after closing.

"You've got to let go," he'd said. "It's a business, not a newborn."

But *Stella + Bean* was her newborn. And she'd built it by hand.

Monday morning. 6:17 AM.

She pulled up and saw the reflection first, the warping of light where the shopfront should've been smooth. The main panel of glass was fractured like a spiderweb, water pooled against the threshold. Inside, the floor was soaked, the power was off, and the mirrored wall menu had peeled halfway from the condensation.

The smell hit her when she opened the door. Damp timber and stale milk. A quiet, watery grief.

She stood there, shoes sinking into soft plywood, staring at the wreckage.

“No problem,” she muttered. “That’s what insurance is for.”

Her broker, Alan, picked up on the first ring.

“Olivia. You okay?”

“Not really. The storm took out the front glass. Water’s inside. Fridge units are gone. Power’s tripped. I’ve got customers due at seven.”

“I’m on it. Give me an hour.”

She tried to mop, but the squeegee wouldn’t bite. The floor gave slightly when she stepped near the counter. That’s when the anxiety started to settle in her chest like cold coffee—dense and bitter.

Alan called back just after 8:00.

“It’s not good news.”

“Go on.”

“You didn’t take the glass extension when we set up the policy. And your lease puts external glass and signage squarely on you. Clause 9.4, if you want to check.”

“What about the water damage?”

“The insurer’s going to argue the water entered through the broken glass, so it won’t be treated as flood, and they’ll say the building wasn’t secure.”

“Business interruption?”

“Not included. You declined it at the time. We discussed premium constraints, remember?”

She sat on the back bench, a soaked rag in her hand, staring at the unplugged espresso machine. The one she'd saved nine months to buy.

"So, I'm not covered for any of this."

"No."

"And you didn't think I should've been warned about the lease clause?"

"I didn't have a copy of the lease, Olivia."

"You never asked."

The repair quote came in by Thursday. Just under $15,000 for the glass. Flooring, electrics, and fridges added another $80,000. Her savings were gone. The bank rejected her loan. Too much short-term risk. She ran a crowdfunding page. Raised $8,200. Not enough.

She closed the doors a month later. No send-off. Just a chalkboard in the window: *Thank you for every cup. We'll miss you.*

Mentor reflection

Olivia didn't lose her café to a storm. She lost it to a gap between the lease and the policy, and to the silence in between.

What if Alan had asked for the lease at the start?
What if he'd flagged the glass extension as essential instead of optional?
What if the quote had included a breakdown: "This is what's covered. This is what's not"?

It's easy to see in hindsight. But your clients don't live in hindsight. They live in the aftermath.

Broker's checklist – lease clause risk review

- Request the full lease before quoting or renewing
- Identify tenant responsibilities: glass, signage, shopfronts, and fit-outs
- Match policy extensions to lease clauses (or document why not)
- Confirm with the client in writing what is excluded by default
- Recommend business interruption coverage for all street-front retail
- Keep file notes, especially where endorsements are declined

Global lens

In 2019, a corner café in Chicago's Lincoln Square district suffered over **USD $250,000** in uninsured damage when wind-blown debris shattered a glass wall during a storm, flooding the premises. The lease placed full responsibility for shopfront maintenance on the tenant. The café had no flood or glass cover and no business interruption insurance. The claim was denied. The business permanently closed two months later.

CPD reflection

- Have you reviewed leases for all client-occupied retail and food businesses?
- Are your SME clients aware that glass and signage are often lease-bound liabilities?
- Are you clearly documenting declined cover options, especially for business interruption?

Chapter 3: Hidden exclusions, hidden loss

"The devil is in the details, but so is salvation."
- Hyman G. Rickover

Real-world case

In 2022, a commercial electronics distributor based in Dallas, Texas lost over **USD $220,000** in uninsured inventory during an overnight warehouse theft. The perpetrators used internal knowledge to access the building without forced entry. The Commercial Package Policy required signs of forcible or violent entry and an active alarm system to trigger coverage. The alarm had been disarmed during a recent system fault and was not reset. The claim was denied. The business lost two major contracts and downsized within the year.

Daniel's story

The silence was the first thing Daniel noticed.

It was 7:42 a.m., and his Dallas warehouse, usually buzzing with clanging bay doors and early freight chatter, was still. Too still. He parked his truck, scanned the perimeter. No broken windows. No visible damage. Just the heat radiating off concrete and a low buzz of something he couldn't yet name.

He unlocked the main entrance. The alarm didn't chirp. His stomach turned.

Inside, the space looked almost untouched, until he stepped farther in and saw the empty shelves. Five whole racks stripped bare. High-end server kits, conference routers, portable projection gear, all gone.

"No," he muttered, moving faster. "No, no, no."

Packing materials lay scattered. A forklift sat idle mid-aisle, ignition off but keys in. A single packing slip drifted across the floor, stamped for a client due to launch a new training campus in San Antonio next week.

His warehouse manager, Antonio, came jogging in a minute later.

"The back door's unlocked," he said, breathless. "No forced entry."

"Alarm?"

"It wasn't armed."

Daniel rubbed the bridge of his nose.

They'd disabled the alarm two weeks ago, system glitch kept triggering false callouts. He'd meant to follow up with the installer. But new contracts, cashflow reports, and client demos had pushed it down the list.

Now it was at the top.

Ruth, his broker, met him within the hour.

"We've got a serious problem," she said, flipping open the claim file on her iPad. "Your policy excludes theft unless there's forcible or violent entry. And it specifies the alarm must be active if installed."

"That can't be it," Daniel said. "We have footage. Someone came in. They took everything."

"But the wording is clear. No sign of break-in, and no armed alarm system, means no cover."

"You said we had full property insurance."

"Full up to the limits of the wording. We discussed crime cover last fall, you said it wasn't worth the extra premium."

Daniel sat on the edge of the nearest packing bench. Dust clung to his palms. His eyes locked on the cracked screen of a dropped handheld scanner on the floor. One of his team must've dropped it during the chaos. Or maybe during the discovery. He couldn't remember hearing it hit the ground.

"I've got $180K in goods gone, and a $140K install next week," he said quietly. "And you're telling me I'm not covered?"

"Not for theft under these conditions."

The claim was denied three days later.

His client, the San Antonio group, cancelled. His distribution contract with a major West Coast supplier was paused pending "business continuity review."

Cashflow cratered. Daniel cut staff hours, moved unsold inventory to a cheaper facility, and started fielding polite refusals from suppliers.

He sold his truck to cover payroll.

When the storage unit invoice came in late the following month, he hesitated before paying it.

The business survived, but just. And it never grew back.

"I didn't get robbed once," he told a friend over beers months later. "I got robbed twice... once by the guy in the warehouse. And once by my own assumptions."

Mentor reflection

Daniel didn't just suffer a theft, he suffered a failure of communication and a blind spot in understanding.

He thought he was covered. His broker thought he understood the policy limits. Neither caught the fact that disabling the alarm would nullify the most critical part of his protection.

What if Ruth had explained the theft conditions with real examples?
What if Daniel had known that one clause, one unchecked box, could gut a six-figure claim?
What if they'd role-played the claim scenario before it happened?

The cost of that conversation is nothing compared to the loss it could've prevented.

Broker's checklist - theft & alarm-based exclusions

- Confirm whether forcible or violent entry is required for theft cover to trigger
- Check policy conditions for operational alarm systems
- Discuss optional crime cover and employee dishonesty endorsements
- Flag high-value inventory or pre-installation exposures requiring review
- Document all coverage declinations and discuss annually
- Provide clients with "If this happened tomorrow..." walkthrough scenarios

Global lens

In 2020, a mid-sized electronics supplier in Birmingham, UK suffered a £190,000 loss when a thief accessed the premises using employee codes. No forced entry occurred. The Combined Commercial Policy required visible signs of break-in and an active monitored alarm. The claim was denied. The business laid off 12 staff and moved into shared premises to survive.

CPD reflection

- Are your clients fully briefed on theft exclusions tied to alarm and entry conditions?
- Have you reviewed coverage differences between basic property cover and crime extensions?
- Would your client know what voids their policy, and would they tell you if they'd done it?

We cover this in my Masterclass module on co-tenancy risks and tenant fit-outs.

Chapter 4: The renovation clause that broke the claim

"To improve is to change, to be perfect is to change often."
- Winston Churchill

Real-world case

In 2021, a lifestyle retailer in Leeds, UK suffered a major ceiling collapse and flood damage during an unnotified shop refurbishment. Contractors had removed sections of plasterboard and ducting without informing the insurer. The Commercial Combined Policy excluded damage from renovations not disclosed in writing. Total losses exceeded **£180,000 (approx. USD $230,000)**. The claim was denied. The store remained closed for 39 days, with permanent revenue loss to competitors.

Alex's story

Alex stood under the dripping light fixture, shoulders tense, as a thin stream of water traced the back wall of his retail space. The air smelled like damp plaster and panic.

The noise had started that morning, just as the first staff member turned on the espresso machine at the café end of the store. A loud crack, then a deep groan, and the ceiling gave way, dumping water and soggy insulation across the front retail section. Merchandise was ruined. Power shorted. Two customers were soaked and startled but unhurt.

The building had seemed fine. Until it wasn't.

He'd renovated a month earlier. Nothing structural, just some lighting and shelving. The contractor had adjusted ducting to fit the new layout and removed part of a redundant ceiling bulkhead. No permits were needed, and no engineers were involved. It had all felt straightforward. Alex hadn't told the landlord. Hadn't told the insurer. Hadn't thought to.

By the time the electrician arrived, water had travelled through four ceiling panels. A stock of wool throws and designer homewares was soaked through. Insurance would sort it, Alex thought. That was what it was for.

The loss adjuster arrived the next day.

“Did you carry out any recent renovations?” she asked.

“Just a refit. Cosmetic. No major changes.”

“Did you notify your broker or the insurer?”

“No. Should I have?”

She raised an eyebrow and jotted something down.

“There’s a clause in your policy. Section 17.2. It excludes any damage arising from unnotified alterations or improvements unless agreed in writing.”

Alex blinked.

“It wasn’t structural.”

“You removed ceiling material and ducting. That qualifies under the clause.”

The next week, his broker confirmed the worst.

“They’re declining the claim. Renovation work voided coverage for the ceiling damage and water ingress. Because it wasn’t disclosed.”

“I thought I had full cover.”

“You did, within the policy wording. We discussed the alteration clause when you first moved in.”

“That was two years ago.”

“I understand.”

“Apparently, I didn’t.”

Repairs cost over £40,000. Lost stock: £28,000. Business interruption: more than £100,000 in missed Christmas trade. The damage came just weeks before his peak season.

Alex took a loan to cover costs. He reopened in February, but the foot traffic never returned to its prior high. A competitor two doors down captured his holiday customers. He laid off one staff member and suspended all future expansion plans.

He now keeps a checklist on his desk: **Notify insurer, always.**

"I didn't just pay for the reno," he said later. "I paid for not knowing what it cost me."

Mentor reflection

The line between cosmetic and structural can be thin. But the line in the policy is not.

Many Commercial Property policies contain clauses that void cover when alterations are made without written disclosure. The wording doesn't care if it was just new lighting, if tradespeople moved ducting, or if no permits were required. If it changes the structure, layout, or systems of the property, it could cost everything.

What if Alex's broker had emailed him every six months to ask, "Any planned works?"
What if his fit-out contractor had flagged the policy clause in the job quote?
What if someone, anyone, had asked the question before the ceiling collapsed?

It's not about blame. It's about missed chances to protect the business.

Broker's checklist – renovation, fit-out and alteration risk

- Ask the client, "Have you made or planned any changes to the premises?"
- Review alteration and works clauses in the current policy wording
- Advise clients of common examples that can void cover: new walls, lighting, HVAC changes
- Notify underwriters of all known renovations or fit-outs, even if minor
- Recommend written client sign-off when cover remains unchanged post-disclosure

- Schedule renovation prompts in renewal reminders or mid-term check-ins

Global lens

In 2022, a health store in Queensland, Australia lost over AUD $140,000 when a new ceiling fan installation caused wiring overload and a subsequent fire. The ISR policy excluded any damage linked to unnotified electrical or structural alterations. The claim was denied. The store reopened three months later at half capacity.

CPD reflection

- Are you asking clients routinely about any recent or upcoming premises alterations?
- Do your clients understand that even "minor" works can impact their cover?
- Have you proactively flagged renovation clauses during policy inception and renewal?

Masterclass

Explore this in my Module on *Renovation disclosures and policy condition traps*, where we cover policy wording triggers, real claim examples, and downloadable checklists for client disclosure conversations. Available now in the Risk Advisor Academy Property & BI Masterclass.

Chapter 5: Sprinkler failure and the hotel flood

"You don't drown by falling in the water. You drown by staying there."
- Edwin Louis Cole

Real-world case

In 2020, a luxury hotel in Melbourne's CBD suffered extensive property and business interruption losses after a faulty sprinkler head activated in a service corridor. The cause was later traced to an undetected valve defect combined with low system pressure. Damage spanned seven floors, impacting multiple suites, lifts, and common areas. The claim exceeded **AUD $6.5 million (approx. USD $4.8 million)**. Delays in maintenance logs, valve replacement schedules, and policy condition reviews led to partial disputes between the insured and insurer, slowing payment and causing reputational harm.

Chris's story

When the water reached the carpet on Level 5, the night manager assumed a pipe had burst in the service hallway. He wasn't entirely wrong.

What no one saw until later was the cascade, sprinkler heads in the east wing had misfired one by one, triggered not by smoke, but by a pressure anomaly that caused the dry valve to open. Cold storage air from the restaurant level had leaked into the ceiling void, warping the mechanism. The result? Forty-five minutes of steady, high-pressure water soaking six guest suites, a corridor, two conference rooms, and the hotel gym.

Chris arrived just after 3:00 a.m., tie off, hair damp from sprinting through the rain.

"Show me the feed," he barked, squinting at the security screen.

Black and white footage showed water flooding past security lights like a sheet of silver. A rolling tide across tile and carpet.

By dawn, four guests had been relocated. One family of VIP travellers had already left for a different hotel, vowing never to return.

Chris stood in the conference hallway, water pooling at the threshold, the faint buzz of a tripped light fixture humming above his head.

“Tell me we’re insured,” he said into the phone.

“We are,” replied the broker. “But the fine print will matter.”

The initial loss assessment landed hard. Water damage to ceilings, plasterboard, electricals, flooring, bedding, and AV systems. Repairs estimated at over AUD $3 million. Business interruption from cancelled conferences and long-lead suite bookings: projected at more than AUD $2.5 million.

But the insurer had questions.

“Was the system maintained in accordance with the policy?”
“Were valve inspections up to date?”
“Was the defect known, or should it have been?”

Chris pulled the maintenance logs himself. The last valve service had been delayed twice, contractor backlog and COVID disruption. No one had flagged it. No one had updated the compliance calendar. The fault hadn’t been known, but it hadn’t been impossible to find, either.

The insurer paid, but not quickly. The investigation dragged. Adjusters questioned every missed line in the logbook. Legal counsel got involved.

Chris’s GM pulled him into a meeting.

“Next time,” she said, “don’t just tell me we’re covered. Show me why we’ll be paid.”

By the time the final settlement came through, the damage had already gone deeper. Conference clients had shifted venues. A national fitness event dropped the hotel for its Sydney rival. The brand damage couldn’t be quantified, but it hurt.

Chris stayed on for another year. Then he moved into private advisory work. He never forgot the flood.

“We weren’t uncovered,” he said later, “but we were unready.”

113

Mentor reflection

Policy conditions are not technicalities; they are the skeleton that holds the claim upright.

When coverage depends on system functionality, maintenance, or compliance, brokers must be proactive in confirming not just that a system exists, but that it's maintained as required. Because when it fails, so does confidence.

What if the broker had asked for the sprinkler maintenance logs at renewal?
What if the hotel had used a shared compliance tracker, rather than scattered contractor notes?
What if someone had tested that valve, even once, in the past six months?

Broker's checklist – sprinkler, system failure and maintenance dependencies

- Review policy conditions tied to active protection systems (sprinklers, alarms, HVAC)
- Confirm with clients whether maintenance is outsourced or internally tracked
- Request maintenance logs at renewal for large property risks
- Advise clients of the impact of deferred or incomplete service intervals
- Document any disclosed gaps, and flag high-risk compliance failures to underwriters
- Encourage integration of compliance calendars and checklists in site walkthroughs

Global lens

In 2021, a luxury hotel in London's Canary Wharf experienced water damage exceeding **£3.8 million (approx. USD $4.6 million)** after a sprinkler head activated due to undiagnosed mechanical vibration. The claim was partially reduced due to delayed maintenance and missed inspections. A key corporate client moved its annual booking to a competitor the following year.

CPD reflection

- Do your commercial property clients rely on active systems that are maintenance-sensitive?
- Are you reviewing their compliance documentation as part of your renewal process?
- How would your clients respond to the question: "Are you confident your systems are up to code?"

Ready to Go Deeper?

By now, you've seen what can go wrong, and what great broking can make right.

If you've been nodding along, thinking *"I want to be the kind of broker who sees these risks before the loss,"* then you're ready for more.

The **Property & Business Interruption Insurance Broker Masterclass** builds on every story in this book with:

- Clause-by-clause policy training
- Real-world case comparisons, both paid and declined
- Walkthroughs of leases, valuations, and asset schedules
- Downloadable tools including templates and calculators
- Global application across Australia, New Zealand, the United States, the United Kingdom, and Canada
- CPD-accredited and regionally aligned learning pathways

Launching late 2025.

Bookmark your access: www.riskadvisoracademy.com
Want early access? Join the waitlist or reach out at:
paul@riskadvisoracademy.com

This book is just the beginning.
The Masterclass is where you build mastery of your profession.

Chapter 6: Stock underdeclared, coverage overestimated

"A small error in the beginning leads to a multitude of errors in the end."
- Aristotle

Real-world case

In 2022, a specialty apparel distributor in Seattle, Washington suffered over **USD $1.8 million** in losses when a three-alarm warehouse fire destroyed their entire seasonal inventory. Their property policy provided blanket cover with a coinsurance clause and values declared at USD $750,000 based on outdated figures. Post-loss review showed stock on hand was over USD $2.2 million. The insurer applied an underinsurance penalty of nearly 65 percent. Final payout: just over USD $900,000. The business survived but was forced to liquidate its holiday contracts and downsize its supply chain for the next fiscal year.

Sarah's story

Sarah walked the scorched perimeter of her warehouse, each step squelching on the damp concrete, the scent of smoke still tangled in the air. Ash from what had once been display-ready winter jackets clung to the soles of her boots.

Two days earlier, she had been prepping for her biggest season yet, Black Friday through Christmas. The racks had been full, the forecasts promising. Her team had pulled a late shift staging orders for national retailers. Now, the racks were twisted steel, and cardboard boxes looked like crumpled black leaves.

"We're insured," she told her operations manager when they arrived that morning. "We're going to be okay."

She had said it with conviction. She had believed it.

Her broker, Greg, arrived by 10:00 a.m., notepad in hand, tie tucked under a windbreaker.

“The adjuster’s en route,” he said. “Can we talk declared values?”

“We’ve got blanket cover, right?” Sarah asked. “One limit across the property.”

“Correct. But the coinsurance clause applies. They’ll assess whether the declared amount reflected your actual exposure.”

“We’re covered to $750K.”

“And your pre-Christmas inventory, what was it worth?”

She hesitated.

“Closer to $2 million, maybe more.”

Greg’s face stiffened.

“You may be subject to a significant penalty. The policy requires you to declare 100 percent of your stock values. The limit wasn’t the issue, it’s the declared value that matters for payout calculations.”

“But we’ve been using that figure for three years.”

“That’s the problem.”

The adjuster confirmed the worst. Actual stock on hand valued at $2.26 million. Declared value? $750,000.

With the 100 percent coinsurance clause in effect, the insurer would only pay a portion of the loss. The underinsurance penalty cut her payout nearly in half.

The total payout: just over $900,000.

It wasn’t enough to rebuild in time for the holidays. Sarah cancelled five major distribution contracts and refunded deposits. Her retail partners replaced her line with competitors. One told her bluntly, *“We can’t risk another no-delivery season.”*

By January, she’d laid off a third of her staff. She liquidated her spring inventory at a loss.

“The fire didn’t sink me,” she told her CPA. “The number I didn’t check did.”

Mentor reflection

Stock values aren't just numbers on a spreadsheet, they are the difference between being made whole and being left behind.

Coinsurance penalties are among the most misunderstood parts of commercial property insurance. Many business owners believe they are fully covered because the policy limit seems high enough. But it's not the limit, it's the declared value that sets the foundation for payout.

What if Greg had asked for a quarterly stock report and matched it against declared values?
What if Sarah had been walked through the coinsurance example at renewal instead of relying on past figures?
What if they had pressure-tested the policy against a total loss scenario?

Broker's checklist - stock declaration, inventory volatility and coinsurance

- Review all policies for coinsurance or average clauses linked to declared values
- Ask clients to provide quarterly or seasonal inventory reports
- Identify seasonal peaks and adjust declared values accordingly
- Provide a worked example of a coinsurance penalty based on underinsurance
- Flag discrepancies between insured limit and expected stock levels
- Document conversations about declaration methodology and value changes

Global lens

In 2021, a mid-size gourmet foods wholesaler in Bristol, UK experienced over £1.2 million in fire damage. Their declared stock value was £450,000. A coinsurance clause triggered an underinsurance penalty of nearly 50 percent. The payout left the business unable to meet supply obligations for their largest distributor, who then terminated their contract. The business filed for insolvency nine months later.

CPD reflection

- Are you educating clients about the difference between policy limits and declared values?
- Have you stress-tested a client's policy against a full stock loss scenario?

- Are your clients clear on how coinsurance clauses affect their payout?

Masterclass

For walkthroughs of coinsurance mechanics, policy wording comparisons, and downloadable inventory declaration templates, explore my module on sum insured structures and coinsurance pitfalls inside the Risk Advisor Academy Property & BI Masterclass.

Chapter 7: Business interruption, broken promise

"It's not the things we don't know that hurt us. It's the things we think we know that just ain't so."
- Mark Twain

Real-world case

In 2019, a restaurant in Bath, UK suffered a serious electrical fire that forced closure for over four months. Although their property policy included business interruption cover, the insured amount was based on gross revenue minus VAT, not on insured gross profit as defined in the policy. The client and broker had misunderstood the basis of declaration. The sum insured fell short by nearly **£500,000 (approx. USD $620,000)**. The payout covered only 57 percent of the loss. The business took out emergency loans and scaled back operations permanently.

Liam's story

The fire didn't look like much from the outside. Just some charred signage, faint smoke curling up the stonework, and a couple of cracked windows.

But inside, *Thorn & Ash* was a different scene.

The blaze had started in a ceiling void above the pastry station. Electrical fault. Flames raced through the ductwork. By the time the fire brigade cleared the site, the refrigeration units were fried, ceilings torn down, and power disconnected for safety. Smoke damage had curled every menu and soaked every bottle label.

Liam arrived to the smell of wet ash and scorched rosemary oil. His head chef was pacing out front, still in a soot-streaked apron.

"We had five weddings booked this month," he said quietly.

Liam nodded, jaw locked tight. He wasn't ready to speak yet.

His broker, Dominic, called within the hour.

"You're covered, Liam. Property and business interruption both included."

"How long's the payout going to take?"

"We'll fast-track it. The important part is, you've got cover for gross profit."

"We declared £1.2 million last year. That should hold."

"We'll confirm once the claim team runs the numbers."

The numbers didn't hold.

Two weeks later, Liam sat in Dominic's office with a spreadsheet open between them.

"They're calculating the loss based on insured gross profit," Dominic explained, "which includes turnover, plus closing stock, less opening stock and variable costs."

"But we declared £1.2 million. That was our revenue."

"Right. But insured gross profit isn't just revenue. It has a specific definition under the policy wording. It excludes variable expenses. Your actual insurable gross profit was £1.8 million."

"So we underdeclared?"

"Yes."

"How much will the penalty be?"

"You'll get a reduced payout, proportional to the underinsurance."

Liam closed his eyes and rubbed his temples.

"I thought we were covered. You never explained this definition."

"It's in the wording."

"I trusted you to translate the wording."

The claim settled at just over £1 million. Losses were £1.75 million. A shortfall of more than £700,000. Liam deferred creditor payments and took out a £300,000 commercial bridge loan. The interest repayments ate into profit margins for two years. His sous-chef left to open her own kitchen down the road.

He never fully expanded again.

“We had the right policy,” he said later. “But we gave it the wrong number.”

Mentor reflection

Business interruption insurance isn’t just about having the coverage; it’s about understanding how that coverage calculates in practice.

Many brokers and client’s default to using revenue or turnover figures. But insured gross profit has a precise definition in policy wordings, and under-declaring it, even unintentionally, results in significant shortfall penalties.

What if Dominic had run through a full BI worksheet at renewal?
What if Liam had understood the difference between gross revenue and insurable profit?
What if the policy included a declaration-linked uplift or margin buffer?
What if the forecast was wrong?

Trend uplift matters. If your client is growing and you insure last year's figures without adjustment, you're not protecting the future, they're exposed.

Train your clients to think forward. Not backward.

Broker's checklist - BI gross profit and underinsurance

- Always use the insurer's definition of "gross profit" (not accounting or tax definitions)
- Walk through a sample BI worksheet with the client before declaring sums insured
- Review the client's accounts or profit & loss report when appropriate
- Include an uplift margin to account for growth and seasonality
- Consider a declaration-linked clause for year-end adjustment
- Explain the potential impact of underinsurance penalties in writing

Global lens

In 2022, a mid-sized bakery distributor in Melbourne, Australia suffered a four-month closure after a gas explosion. Their business interruption cover had a declared gross profit of AUD $1.5 million. Actual gross profit at time of loss was AUD $2.4 million. A coinsurance penalty of 37.5 percent applied. The payout shortfall forced permanent restructuring of their delivery model and staff reductions.

CPD reflection

- Are you confident your clients know what "gross profit" means in insurance terms?
- Are you reviewing financials or P&L reports before finalising BI sums insured?
- How clearly are you communicating the risks of underinsurance on BI policies?

Logging Your CE Or CPD & Putting It into Practice

By now, you've read stories that hit close to home, losses that could've been avoided, and wins earned through diligence and good advice.

If you're reading this book as part of your professional development, you're already on the right path. To get the most from it:

CE & CPD logging made easy

Most leading broker associations, including NIBA, IBANZ, CII, BIBA, CIAB and others, accept **self-directed CE or CPD** for structured educational reading.

You can use this book to claim time spent learning, reflecting, and applying knowledge.

- **Suggested time:** 4–6 CPD hours
- **CE or CPD category:** Technical / Placement Strategy / Claims Management
- **How to log:** Use the CPD prompts at the end of each chapter to support your self-assessment
- **Format:** Reading, written reflection, and completion of structured workbook activities

About the companion workbook

To support your development, we've created the **Fire, Flood, Failure - Broker Reflection Workbook**, designed to help you bridge the gap between theory and real-world practice.

The workbook includes:

- All 22 CE & CPD reflection prompts
- Guided fields to apply each chapter to your client portfolio
- A printable CE & CPD activity log for your records and compliance audits

Available soon via the Property & BI Masterclass Launchpad

Bookmark your access: www.riskadvisoracademy.com
Sign up to be notified when it goes live — anticipated in late 2025

Tip: Real learning happens through action

Take a moment to pause.

- Which chapter reminded you of a real client?
- Which gap have you seen before—and walked past?
- Where are your assumptions hiding risk?

Use the workbook to map your next move, and carry it into your next renewal, proposal, or placement conversation.

Chapter 8: The cold storage catastrophe

"You think compliance is expensive? Try non-compliance."
- Paul McNulty

Real-world case

In 2020, a refrigerated logistics company in Brisbane, Australia suffered an ammonia leak in its cold storage facility during an unplanned system test. The leak contaminated the stock and forced the shutdown of three warehouse zones. Although property insurance covered structural damage, spoilage was only covered under a separate deterioration of stock extension, which had lapsed at renewal. Total loss exceeded **AUD $1.1 million**. The claim was denied for stock-related losses. The company had to reimburse clients for spoiled goods and lost two long-term distribution contracts.

Jason's story

The call came at 2:47 a.m.

Jason rolled over, already bracing.

"This is Matt," came the voice on the other end. "We've had a leak in Bay 3. Temperature's rising. I think it's the ammonia valve again."

Jason sat up, heart pounding.

"Evacuate. Shut the zone down. I'll be there in ten."

He lived twenty minutes away. Made it in twelve.

The air hit him like bleach when he opened the bay door. The whine of a shutdown compressor echoed through the walls. A red LED screen blinked warnings about coolant pressure.

He pulled on gloves and a mask. Inside, the metal racking sweated with condensation. Plastic tubs of frozen seafood were already beading moisture.

"How long's it been exposed?" he asked the team leader.

"At least ninety minutes. The valve blew during the system test. Auto-restart failed."

Jason had inherited the business from his father, *Southern Reef Distribution*, and modernised it with AI-cooled systems and remote sensors. But some of the legacy units hadn't been upgraded. The ammonia loop in Bay 3 was one of them.

The inspection last month had flagged it. He'd postponed the repair to Q1. Budgets were tight.

By 6:00 a.m., the temperature in Bay 3 had risen past the threshold. Pallets of high-value perishable seafood had lost integrity. Over **$800,000** in goods spoiled, including a specialty tuna shipment bound for Tokyo and frozen lobster stock for a nationwide supplier.

Jason walked the line of crates. Some lids had cracked. Others were sweating like stones left in the sun. He clenched his jaw.

"Insurance will cover the loss," he said.

Except it didn't.

His broker, Aimee, returned his call mid-morning.

"I've spoken to the insurer," she said. "The good news is property damage is covered. Compressor and valve repair included."

"And the stock?"

"The deterioration of stock extension was removed at last renewal."

"Removed?"

"Yes. It wasn't selected as part of the updated cover. We discussed cutting it to reduce premium."

"I don't remember that conversation."

"It's in my notes. We can revisit it."

"A little late."

The claim for damaged equipment was accepted, $112,000.

The $800,000 stock loss? Declined.

Jason had to reimburse his customers. One cancelled their annual contract. Another demanded tighter delivery guarantees or threatened legal action. Jason dipped into the business line of credit to cover short-term payments.

The upgraded system was finally installed, but at half capacity. Expansion plans for the southern corridor were shelved. He didn't sleep through the night again for months.

"The stock wasn't just lost," he told a peer at a conference. "It was uninsured. Because I let the conversation stop at saving cost."

Mentor reflection

Stock cover for perishables isn't just about whether it's included, it's about whether the right **extension** is active.

Policies often separate building damage from spoilage or contamination losses. And brokers may assume the client understands the structure of their cover. But when the freezer breaks down, and the prawns start to thaw, there's no time left for fine print.

What if Aimee had flagged the specific value at risk, and tested the scenario?
What if Jason had reviewed all removed extensions with his operations manager?
What if they'd simulated a total freezer failure, just once, during renewal?

Broker's checklist - cold storage, stock deterioration and operational cover

- Review all cold storage and refrigerated risks for spoilage exposure
- Confirm if the deterioration of stock is included as a separate extension
- Clarify the difference between structural equipment cover and stock-related loss
- Identify any legacy or outdated systems with known risks
- Document any removed extensions and the rationale in writing

- Offer claim simulations at renewal to highlight risk exposure

Global lens

In 2021, a frozen food distributor in Chicago lost over **USD $1.4 million** when a power surge knocked out their refrigeration systems over a holiday weekend. The building was covered under the BOP policy, but the spoilage extension had not been renewed due to oversight. The claim for stock was denied. The distributor lost a national grocer contract and spent the next year rebuilding trust.

CPD reflection

- Are you confirming with clients what's **not** covered under default property wordings?
- Have you walked clients through spoilage or contamination extensions, particularly with cold storage?
- Are you maintaining clear records when cover is declined or removed for cost reasons?

Chapter 9: The fit-out that sank the schedule

"It's not the load that breaks you, it's the way you carry it."
- Lou Holtz

Real-world case

In 2022, a fast-casual restaurant chain in Portland, Oregon suffered over **USD $850,000** in uninsured losses after a kitchen fire destroyed their flagship location. Although the property policy covered building damage, the client's high-end custom fit-out, including imported kitchen lines, seating, and lighting, was not correctly scheduled. The standard improvements clause had a cap of USD $250,000. The broker had not requested a detailed asset schedule, and the insured had not realised their lease-required improvements were their responsibility to insure. The claim was only partially paid. The site remained closed for over nine months.

Jordan's story

Jordan arrived to find fire crews packing up and the scent of scorched wood clinging to the sidewalk. His flagship venue, Mesa Junction, was now a blackened shell. It had won sustainability awards, graced local magazines, drawn investors. He stood motionless, watching water drain from a cracked mosaic tile, the last detail he remembered installing by hand.

The fire had started in a wall-mounted oven. An electrical short. Staff had evacuated quickly, but flames spread through the ducting and raced through the timber slats. By the time suppression systems kicked in, it was too late.

"It's a write-off," the fire captain said.

Jordan didn't answer. His eyes were locked on the twisted remains of the handmade copper bar.

Six months earlier, the fit-out had cost him everything: equity from a second location, a business loan, and hundreds of unpaid hours. He'd assumed, no, trusted, it was insured. That's what property insurance was for.

"We're covered, right?" he asked his broker, Erin, the next day.

"The landlord's policy covers the shell," she said. "You're responsible for improvements."

"That's in the lease, yes... but we have coverage."

"You didn't submit a fit-out schedule. The policy only applies the unscheduled tenant improvements clause, capped at $250,000."

"You didn't ask me for one."

"It's standard. We recommend it, but without details, we can't schedule values."

"I assumed the limit reflected my investment."

"And I assumed you'd flag anything major."

The insurer paid out $250,000. Jordan's actual loss was more than triple that.

He delayed vendor payments, deferred payroll, and liquidated his second location's backup stock to stay afloat. A key investor withdrew. His builder filed for partial default when materials couldn't be paid on time.

Mesa Junction reopened 11 months later. But by then, the buzz was gone.

"We didn't lose the fire," Jordan later said. "We lost the fit-out, and we lost time. And in this business, time is reputation."

Mentor reflection

Fit-outs are often a tenant's most significant investment—and yet the most underinsured.

Tenants frequently assume their improvements are automatically covered, especially in spaces they don't own. But unless scheduled explicitly, most policies cap cover at a general improvements limit. A single oven or architectural element can exceed that on its own.

What if Erin had provided a templated asset register and reviewed the lease together with Jordan?
What if Jordan had asked for a mock claim walkthrough at renewal?

The difference between a minor delay and a brand-breaking shutdown can be one overlooked clause.

Broker's checklist – fit-outs, improvements and schedule mismatches

- Review lease clauses to confirm tenant fit-out obligations
- Ask clients to complete a full asset register with supporting values
- Flag the cap on unscheduled improvements clauses in policy terms
- Provide fit-out examples from similar businesses to spark memory
- Document any schedule omissions and client assumptions in writing
- Encourage regular review of the improvement schedule for inflation or upgrades

Global lens

In 2021, a boutique café in Glasgow, UK lost over £420,000 in uninsured fit-out costs after a gas leak caused an explosion. The policy had a £100,000 improvements cap. The remaining assets were never declared. The business reopened a year later in a reduced format with a new brand.

CPD reflection

- Do your clients understand the difference between property cover and declared improvements?
- Are you providing templates or support in building asset registers?
- Would you be confident defending your advice if a claim denial landed?

Masterclass

Learn more in my module on co-tenancy exposures and fit-out schedules, including annotated lease reviews and editable asset register templates, inside the Risk Advisor Academy Property & BI Masterclass.

Chapter 10: Flooded by assumption

"Assumptions are the termites of relationships."
- Henry Winkler

Real-world case

In 2021, a boutique homewares retailer in York, UK suffered **£480,000 (approx. USD $590,000)** in damages when surface water flooding surged through the back entrance during a major rain event. The client believed flood was covered. However, the policy excluded surface water and overland flow unless added by endorsement. The broker had marked the risk low based on postcode, and the extension was never discussed. The claim was denied. The business operated from a temporary location for six months and lost key wholesale suppliers.

Elise's story

Elise was folding linen throws when the water came in. It started as a trickle, then pushed through the back corridor like a slow-moving tide. The storm drains in the alley had overflowed, forcing muddy runoff under the back threshold.

She shouted to her assistant. Towels, crates, anything to block the doors.

But it was too late.

By the time the worst passed, nearly half the showroom was under water. Dozens of handwoven rugs and artisan ceramics were ruined. The storeroom smelled like wet timber and varnish.

Her broker, Edward, called back around 4:00 p.m.

"You're covered for storm," he said.

"It wasn't storm. It was runoff. Surface water."

"Elise... your policy excludes flood unless it's endorsed."

"Flood? No one said flood wasn't covered."

"You're in a low-risk zone. We didn't include it."

"I never declined it."

"And I never quoted it."

Silence.

"I assumed it was in there."

"So did I."

The claim for damage and interruption was denied. Elise salvaged what she could and moved to a borrowed shopfront nearby. Her wholesaler cancelled their next seasonal contract. She withdrew from the Birmingham trade show.

By winter, foot traffic was down 40 percent.

"It wasn't the water that took us under," she said later. "It was the silence between what we should have said."

Mentor reflection

Flood exclusions are subtle but devastating.

Most policies treat storm and flood as separate perils. Surface water and overland flow may not trigger coverage unless endorsed. A missed clause, a wrongly assumed inclusion, or a skipped conversation can cost hundreds of thousands.

What if Edward had explained storm versus flood in plain terms?
What if Elise had asked what wasn't covered?
What if the word "assumed" had never entered the room?

Broker's checklist – flood cover, surface water and storm wording traps

- Clarify storm vs. flood in every new business and renewal conversation

- Review postcode assumptions against site-specific risks like topography and drainage
- Provide visual examples to show clients the difference in claim outcomes
- Always offer flood as a quoted extension, even if low-risk
- Document any decline or omission clearly, including rationale
- Use real claims to explain consequences of exclusion

Global lens

In 2022, a family-run kitchen supply store in Sydney, Australia suffered over **AUD $700,000** in damages when overland flow breached the basement. Storm cover was active, but flood was excluded under the ISR policy. The claim was denied. The business lost major contracts and scaled back operations.

CPD reflection

- Do you quote and explain flood extensions even in "low-risk" zones?
- Have you mapped surface water exclusions in policy wordings for different insurers?
- Could your clients explain their flood position clearly in a crisis?

Chapter 11: The lease clause that cut the claim

"A small detail overlooked often becomes the biggest regret."
- Winston Churchill

Real-world case

In 2020, a mid-sized law firm in Bristol, UK was forced to temporarily cease operations when a burst pipe from an upstairs tenant caused major damage to their leased office space. Although their property policy included business interruption cover, the lease required the landlord, not the tenant, to reinstate the premises following insured damage. The broker and client both assumed that the BI cover would trigger immediately. However, due to the landlord's delays and lack of alignment between the lease and the policy, the firm's BI claim was limited to three months of indemnity, well short of the nine months it took for reinstatement. The remaining claim was denied, as the insured had no insurable interest in the rebuild timeline.

Loss of income: £780,000. Several clients moved to competitors. A partner later resigned.

Naomi's story

Naomi pulled into the carpark at 7:58 a.m., rain whispering on the windshield. She was always the first in, senior partner or not.

The water was visible before she unlocked the door. A trail along the hall, thick as spilled paint, led toward the boardroom. She kicked off her shoes and stepped forward.

It was raining inside.

A ceiling tile dropped with a soft thud, followed by another. Bookshelves soaked through. The carpet felt like a sponge. Computers glinted from behind puddled glass.

Upstairs, the neighbouring café had suffered a burst pipe overnight. The water had crept down between walls and into ceilings, soaking Naomi's entire office floor.

Her broker, Dominic, arrived before the insurers.

"You've got BI on the policy," he said. "Twelve months."

"The lease says the landlord is responsible for repairs."

"Right. But BI will trigger during the rebuild."

"Even though I'm not the one rebuilding?"

"That's correct. Your revenue's impacted. You've got cover."

But two months later, the insurer had a different view.

"The indemnity period started at the date of damage," the loss adjuster explained. "But you didn't begin repairs."

"I can't," Naomi said. "It's not my building. It's the landlord's."

"Then you've no insurable interest in the reinstatement."

"So my BI cover..."

"Only applies while your business is impacted by insured damage to your property interest. The longer delay is contractual."

"But we didn't cause the delay."

"And your policy didn't cover for it."

They received three months of lost income. After that, the insurer declined to extend coverage. The landlord took nine months to complete works. Naomi's team worked from home, but it wasn't the same. A major client left during the disruption. Another firm moved into their former lease space before she could sign a renewal.

"It wasn't just the pipe," she said later. "It was the clause that meant we couldn't start again."

Mentor reflection

BI isn't just about cover, it's about control.

A common trap is assuming that business interruption cover "automatically" runs until the business recovers. But if the insured party isn't the one controlling the rebuild, or worse, has no insurable interest in it, the policy may not respond beyond a basic indemnity period.

Naomi's lease made the landlord responsible for reinstatement. But the policy didn't reflect that dependency, and her broker didn't flag the exposure. As a result, when the landlord delayed, the BI cover stopped short, legitimately.

What if Dominic had reviewed the lease with Naomi?
What if they'd considered a longer indemnity period, or a dependency extension?
What if the cover had been structured to reflect what Naomi *couldn't control*?

Broker's checklist – BI cover vs lease obligations

- Always request a copy of the lease (or relevant clauses) when structuring BI
- Identify who is responsible for repairs or reinstatement under the lease
- Ensure indemnity period is aligned to the **slowest party in control**
- Where landlord is responsible, confirm insured interest is structured appropriately
- Consider adding wording for **delayed access, landlord reinstatement**, or **premises not ready** clauses
- Review the interplay between fit-out insurance and premises control

Global lens

In 2022, a dental clinic in Melbourne, Australia suffered a ceiling collapse due to a leaking roof in their leased space. The landlord was slow to repair the premises, and the clinic's BI cover was structured around a 6-month indemnity period. Repairs took 13 months. The insurer declined the second half of the claim. The practice lost key staff and dropped below break-even for nearly a year.

CPD reflection

- Do you assess the lease for control and reinstatement terms before structuring BI?
- Are you helping your clients understand how indemnity periods connect to repair timelines?
- Would your policy wording respond if your client isn't the one reinstating the premises?

Masterclass

Explore this in more detail in my module on renovation disclosures and policy condition traps, including annotated lease reviews, dependency exposure guides, and tailored BI structuring tips, inside the Risk Advisor Academy Property & BI Masterclass.

Chapter 12: The deductible that drowned the claim

"It's not what you know that gets you in trouble. It's what you know for sure that just ain't so."
- Mark Twain

Real-world case

In 2021, a luxury furniture importer based in Brisbane, Australia experienced a major loss when floodwaters entered their warehouse during an extreme weather event. The company had recently raised their ISR deductible from $10,000 to $100,000 to reduce their annual premium. They believed it was a manageable risk. But the total loss to stock and flooring came to just under $97,000, below their deductible. The claim was denied in full, and the business was left to absorb the entire loss. Compounding the issue, the firm did not understand that the same $100,000 deductible would apply to any Business Interruption claim as well, had it triggered.

The shortfall stalled their next shipment, lost a retail partner, and delayed expansion plans by over a year.

Darren's story

Darren stood ankle-deep in water that smelled of plywood and varnish. His entire ground floor was submerged. Couches bobbed against pallets, and rolls of designer fabric leaned like felled trees.

He'd known the rains were coming. He'd even moved the most expensive stock to the mezzanine. But the storm drains failed again, and the flash flood rose faster than expected.

By noon, he'd stopped hoping it would recede. By four, he'd called his broker.

"We're under," he said. "Probably eighty to ninety thousand in damage."

"Okay," the broker replied. "Let me pull the policy. You're on the higher deductible now, right?"

"We raised it last year to save costs. Went to a hundred."

"Then unfortunately, this won't be a claim."

"But it's a massive hit..."

"It's under your deductible. Insurer won't respond."

"We've never claimed before! We've paid thousands in premiums."

"That's... how deductibles work. They're your skin in the game."

The insurer confirmed the loss estimate: $96,840. Clean-up, disposal, restocking, reordering from overseas, all on Darren.

Worse, he discovered that if the water damage had caused a prolonged closure, the same $100,000 deductible would have applied to his Business Interruption cover, too, per claim. Not pro rata.

He cancelled a planned showroom expansion. A retail partner pulled out after delays in order fulfilment. Two staff left during the uncertainty.

"If I'd known I was betting the business to save $3,000 in premium," he said later, "I'd have found the money elsewhere."

Mentor reflection

Deductibles (or excesses) are not just accounting lines, they're strategic decisions.

Raising the deductible can reduce premiums, yes, but only if the client understands what they're giving up. In Darren's case, a high deductible removed protection from the very type of mid-tier loss most likely to occur.

Even worse, many clients and some brokers don't realise that the same deductible can apply to **multiple sections**, including BI, sometimes as an **aggregate**, sometimes **per section**, and sometimes **per claim**.

What if Darren's broker had run a loss threshold analysis?
What if he'd explained BI deductibles separately?
What if the risk saving had been aligned to the stock levels on site?

Broker's checklist – structuring deductibles and retentions

- Always explain deductible structures in both dollar and risk terms
- Provide clients with examples of losses that would and would not be claimable
- Clarify if deductibles apply per event, per section, or per claim
- Review BI deductibles, which are often misunderstood and sometimes uncapped
- Ensure deductible strategy matches cashflow and risk tolerance, not just premium savings
- Discuss aggregate vs. per-loss deductibles for complex or multi-site clients

Global lens

In 2019, a tech accessory distributor in Toronto, Canada, increased their deductible from $25,000 to $250,000 as part of a hard market premium negotiation. Later that year, a warehouse theft caused $220,000 in losses, entirely under deductible. The insurer denied the claim. The firm could not recover its Q4 revenue and exited two product lines the following year.

CPD reflection

- Are your clients aware of how deductibles impact small and mid-size claims?
- Can you explain the deductible application across Property, BI, and Additional Costs?
- Have you helped clients model the tipping point between savings and retained risk?

Masterclass

Dig deeper into deductible structuring and BI application scenarios in my module on structuring for affordability and control, including walkthroughs of deductible selection strategies, flood-exposed client examples, and retention modeling templates, available in the Risk Advisor Academy Property & BI Masterclass.

Chapter 13: The timeline they never tested

"Plans are useless, but planning is everything."
- Dwight D. Eisenhower

Real-world case

In 2022, a specialty kitchen manufacturer in New Jersey, USA suffered a fire that destroyed their main production facility. The Business Interruption coverage had a 12-month indemnity period, considered "standard" by both client and broker. However, the site required zoning approval, custom machinery reorders, and workforce rehiring. The actual time to rebuild and return to pre-loss revenue levels: 19 months. The policy only responded for 12 months. The final $1.3 million in lost income was uninsured.

The business survived, but took on high-interest debt, lost its CFO, and failed to win a key retail distribution contract in the aftermath.

Aaron's story

The fire took everything except the loading dock.

Aaron stood on the edge of the rubble at sunrise, arms crossed against the cold. It smelled like scorched aluminum and melted circuit boards. One week earlier, he'd been planning a product launch. Now, he was wondering if he still had a business.

Insurance adjusters came. Engineers measured beams. His broker assured him the Business Interruption policy would carry them through. Aaron trusted that, until month thirteen.

"I thought we had twelve months of cover," he said.

"We do," the broker replied.

"But we're still down thirty percent in revenue. Clients are slow to return. Marketing's still catching up. The new CNC rig just arrived."

"Twelve months is the indemnity period. The policy doesn't cover beyond that."

"Even if we're not back?"

"Even then."

"But we only just reopened. The rebuild took almost eleven months."

"It's about time from *damage*, not reopening."

Aaron reviewed his old quotes later. The broker had offered 12 or 18 months. He'd chosen 12. The price difference had seemed small but so had the risk.

Now he was explaining to investors why the last $1.3 million in projected revenue wouldn't be covered, and why hiring was frozen.

"We planned for the event," Aaron said later. "We never tested the timeline."

Mentor reflection

Indemnity period selection is one of the **most consequential choices** in BI cover, and one of the most misunderstood.

Many clients assume that "twelve months" means "until we're back." But the indemnity period starts from **date of damage**, not from when the rebuild begins or when customers return.

A twelve-month period might be enough—for simple fit-outs, quick rebuilds, or businesses with no brand exposure. But manufacturing? Regulated premises? Bespoke equipment? Delayed customer recovery? Every one of these stretches the timeline.

What if Aaron had modeled the rebuild stages in advance?
What if the broker had walked him through a loss timeline simulation?
What if someone had asked: "what would you need to be fully back?"

Broker's checklist – indemnity period and BI recovery lag

- Start BI planning with a timeline, not a policy limit

- Consider rebuild time, regulatory approvals, equipment delays, staffing, and customer return lag
- Don't rely on "industry standard", tailor to the client's operation
- Distinguish between **property reinstatement** and **business recovery**
- Use real-life rebuild case examples to challenge assumptions
- Offer 24-month quotes as default for clients with rebuild exposure

Global lens

In 2020, a custom optics manufacturer in Nottingham, UK suffered a facility fire. They had a 12-month BI indemnity period. Between custom glass refits, ISO compliance re-certification, and staff recruitment delays, the business didn't return to pre-loss revenue for 17 months. The insurer paid out for only 12. The remaining £620,000 in losses were absorbed or financed.

CPD reflection

- Do you start BI conversations with a timeline or a quote?
- Are you confident clients understand the true duration of their recovery?
- Could you defend a 12-month indemnity period in court, or to an auditor?

Masterclass

Explore this deeper in my module on indemnity period structuring and revenue lag modeling, including real loss timelines, claim case studies, and visual client tools—available inside the Risk Advisor Academy Property & BI Masterclass.

Chapter 14: The missing link in the chain

"The strength of a chain is measured by its weakest link."
- Thomas Reid

Real-world case

In 2018, a precision metal parts manufacturer in Yorkshire, UK experienced a sudden halt in production, not because of internal damage, but because their sole supplier's warehouse caught fire. The raw materials needed to fulfil two major contracts were lost. The client's own facility was unharmed, and their broker had not structured any form of Dependent or Contingent Business Interruption (CBI) cover. The resulting loss of revenue exceeded £1.1 million. Their customer sued for late delivery, and the business laid off a third of its workforce.

Leo's story

Leo stared at the email for a full ten seconds before reacting.
"We've had a fire," it read. **"Our stock's gone. We're down for the next six weeks minimum."**

The supplier was a small but critical cog in Leo's aerospace fabrication chain. They supplied a unique aluminium alloy extrusion, tailored to his specs. Without it, nothing else moved.

He called them immediately. They were apologetic. Devastated, even.

"It was an electrical fire. Total loss. We're just thankful no one was hurt."

But that didn't change what was coming.

Two contracts, one with a US military subcontractor, the other with a major German aeronautics firm, were dependent on product delivery that now wouldn't happen. Not on time, not in spec, not without massive retooling.

Leo's broker was next.

"We've had a supplier fire. I'm shut down. We need to activate the BI."

"I'll get the policy. Wait, was the fire at *your* premises?"

"No. Our facility's fine."

"Then the BI doesn't apply. There's no direct damage to your premises."

"But we *can't* operate."

"Unless you've got Dependent BI or CBI wording in place..."

"I don't know. Did you include it?"

Silence.

"The cover assumed we'd be the ones to burn," Leo said later. "We weren't. But we burned all the same."

The fallout came fast. His production backlog grew. One client threatened breach. The other cancelled outright. His creditor tightened terms. Leo had to lay off 19 people, including two engineers he'd trained from apprentices.

Mentor reflection

Business Interruption cover usually responds to **physical damage at the insured's premises**, but modern business doesn't end at your own door.

Today's clients rely on **third-party infrastructure**: manufacturers, distributors, processors, even tech platforms. If those dependencies go down, your client can lose income without ever suffering a fire or flood themselves.

CBI (Contingent BI) or **dependent premises cover** is not automatic. It must be requested, structured, and priced in. Many brokers forget, or never ask, about supply chain risk. Worse, clients rarely volunteer the fact that a single vendor might hold the key to their operations.

What if Leo's broker had mapped out his dependencies?
What if a simple endorsement had added his key suppliers?
What if the policy had reflected how the business *actually* worked?

Broker's checklist – supply chain & dependent premises risks

- Identify key suppliers, manufacturers, and upstream dependencies

- Ask clients: “What if this vendor went offline for 3 months?”
- Consider CBI endorsements for critical third parties
- Review contract terms—some clients may have **delivery penalties** that magnify risk
- Explain that BI without property damage is a **coverage gap**, not a fault in the policy
- Include wording for **named dependencies**, or explore blanket supplier extensions where available

Global lens

In 2021, a specialist cosmetics distributor in Los Angeles, USA faced a six-month loss of income after their main contract manufacturer suffered a flood. The distributor had no CBI cover. Despite having product orders lined up, they had nothing to ship, and no claim to lodge. BI didn’t respond. The business lost a critical retail contract and had to rebrand to survive.

CPD reflection

- Have you mapped your client’s operational dependencies, not just physical premises?
- Do you know which suppliers or vendors are “irreplaceable” in under 60 days?
- Are you comfortable explaining the difference between **BI** and **CBI** in plain English?

Chapter 15: The distribution deal that didn’t deliver

“The supply chain is only as strong as its most obscure link.”
- Nassim Nicholas Taleb

Real-world case

In 2020, a regional beverage manufacturer in Victoria, Australia experienced a sharp drop in revenue after their exclusive national distributor suffered a warehouse fire. The manufacturer’s own premises were unharmed, but with the distributor offline for five months, orders halted and stock sat idle. The manufacturer’s Business Interruption policy responded only to physical damage at their own premises. There was no dependent customer or reverse Contingent BI cover in place. The loss of revenue exceeded $1.2 million, and two state-based sales teams were disbanded.

Olivia’s story

When Olivia’s phone buzzed, she was at a supplier tasting event, pouring their new passionfruit and lime mix into paper cups.

The text was short:
“Warehouse fire. Total loss. Can’t distribute. Will call.”

Her first thought wasn’t panic, it was logistics. Where will we store this week’s run? How do we get product into Queensland without them?

Their national distribution partner had handled everything, warehousing, freight, invoicing. Olivia’s company focused on blending, branding, and bottling.

Without a distributor, the entire system stalled. Orders couldn’t be fulfilled. Promotions were paused. Two major supermarket chains suspended new listings due to uncertainty.

"We're still producing," Olivia told her broker. "But revenue's stopped. We need to trigger the BI."

"Was your facility damaged?"

"No, it's our distributor's site that burned."

"Then the BI won't respond. There's no damage at your location."

"But we can't sell. We're bleeding."

"Unless you had a reverse dependency extension..."

"Did we?"

"I don't think it was selected."

The claim didn't proceed. The stock remained in limbo. Olivia rented emergency warehousing in Sydney at premium rates and tried to self-distribute. It was inefficient, under-resourced, and chaotic.

By the time the distributor returned to operations, two of Olivia's largest clients had found alternate suppliers.

"It wasn't our fire," she said later. "But it became our loss."

Mentor reflection

BI policies generally require **physical damage to the insured's premises** to trigger cover. But for many businesses, especially producers and manufacturers, the risk lies downstream.

A warehouse, key customer, or distributor suffering a fire can choke revenue even if your client's own property is untouched.

This is known as **reverse Contingent Business Interruption** (reverse CBI), or sometimes **unscheduled customer premises exposure**. It's not automatic. It must be structured.

Brokers who don't ask "Where does the money come from?" or "Who handles your orders?" often miss this risk.

What if Olivia's broker had mapped the customer pipeline?
What if the BI policy had a customer premises extension?
What if warehousing and logistics exposure had been included in the risk review?

Broker's checklist - reverse CBI and distribution exposure

- Identify downstream distribution partners and key customer premises
- Ask: "Where would your income stop if a third party went offline?"
- Include reverse CBI or dependent customer premises cover where available
- Explore unscheduled premises extensions for blanket cover
- Model warehouse, logistics, and channel disruption scenarios
- Be alert to single-point-of-failure risks in a client's sales or fulfillment chain

Global lens

In 2022, a California-based organic snack manufacturer lost 40% of their Q3 revenue when a major West Coast grocery chain suffered a distribution center fire. The manufacturer's BI coverage did not include customer premises exposure. The insurer denied the claim. It took over nine months to restore full sales flow, and the company had to sell off expired stock at a loss.

CPD reflection

- Do you ask clients where their revenue truly comes from, not just where they operate?
- Can you distinguish between CBI, reverse CBI, and unscheduled premises coverage?
- Could a loss at a warehouse or retailer devastate your client without triggering a claim?

Covered further in the Masterclass BI extensions module.

A good architect doesn't just draw lines. They see the whole structure before the first brick is laid."
- Frank Gehry

You've come a long way.

By now, you've seen how fires start without flames, how leases hide landmines, and how rebuilding a business is often harder than repairing a building. You've stood beside brokers who got it wrong, and watched clients suffer because of what wasn't known, asked, or insured.

You've also seen what great broking can do. The right question at the right time. The subtle clause that changes everything. The forward-thinking structure that saves a business, a legacy, a livelihood.

What lies ahead are the most complex lessons, cases where even experienced brokers pause. These aren't just policy missteps. They're strategic failures in how coverage was architected.
And that's the key word now: **architecture**.

Great brokers don't just place insurance.
They design coverage structures.
They translate business risk into protection.
They anticipate interdependencies, limits, thresholds, and timelines.
They craft policies that hold under stress, across jurisdictions, layers, and multiple moving parts.

In the next set of chapters, you'll enter that world.

You'll see how layered placements collapse under deductibles.
How subrogation gaps lead to dead ends.
How the wrong audit clause can claw back a client's future.
And how contractual conditions, when misaligned, can undo everything.

These stories are harder.
The stakes are higher.
But so is the reward, for brokers who choose to build like architects.

If you've made it this far, you're not here for surface knowledge.
You're here for mastery.
Let's go further.

Chapter 16: One clause, two cities

"The devil is in the details - but so is the salvation."
- Hyman G. Rickover

Real-world case

In 2021, a national signage and lighting firm headquartered in Ontario, Canada suffered a major fire at their Edmonton manufacturing hub. Although their Industrial Special Risks (ISR) policy covered all locations, the sublimits and deductibles varied by site. The Edmonton location had a $1 million sublimit and a $250,000 deductible, versus $5 million and $50,000 for Ontario. The broker had assumed the higher limits applied everywhere. They did not. The fire loss totaled $1.8 million. The claim was capped at $1 million, and the client absorbed the rest.

It took two years to financially recover. A planned west coast expansion was cancelled. Several key staff relocated.

Arjun's story

The smoke had long cleared, but the damage wasn't over.

Arjun sat in the conference room of their Ontario head office, scrolling through yet another email chain from the insurer. He could almost hear the tone behind the adjuster's words:

"As per your policy's Location Schedule and corresponding Endorsement 3..."

The rest was noise. Legal noise. Expensive noise.

The fire at their Edmonton plant had shut down production on a key national contract. They'd built the signage systems for a major petrol brand, everything from LED pylons to pump toppers.

"We'll be fine," his broker had said the morning after. "Your ISR covers everything."

"Limits okay?" Arjun had asked. "We upgraded the machinery out there last year."

"You're fine. It's a group policy."

But they weren't fine.

A $1.8 million loss. And only $1 million in cover for that site. Worse, a $250,000 deductible, buried in a footnote of the endorsement. They'd been insured, but not equally.

"It's one business," Arjun said. "How can one part be underinsured?"

"Each site had its own limits," the broker admitted. "I didn't realise the Edmonton schedule wasn't updated."

"But we're a national operation. We work as one."

"The policy doesn't."

The remaining $800,000 had to be financed. The petrol client moved their next contract to a competitor. Arjun cancelled an expansion project and reassigned staff from Alberta to Ontario.

"We weren't just missing coverage," he said later. "We were misaligned."

Mentor reflection

Multi-site operations often use composite ISR or All Risks wordings, but that doesn't mean the coverage is uniform.

Each location can have:

- Separate declared values
- Distinct deductibles
- Unique sublimits
- Location-specific endorsements or exclusions

If one site is underdeclared, poorly scheduled, or overlooked during renewal, the policy may respond unevenly, or not at all.

Brokers must **review site-by-site schedules**, reconcile upgrades or asset changes, and ensure endorsements match operational reality.

What if Arjun's broker had aligned sublimits across all key sites?
What if the new machinery had triggered a schedule update?
What if location-specific clauses were cross-checked annually?

Broker's checklist – multi-site policies and ISR schedules

- Confirm all locations are listed, current, and valued appropriately
- Review sublimits, deductibles, and endorsements per site, not just the master policy
- Watch for automatic limitation clauses (e.g., "per premises")
- Update ISR schedules following equipment, stock, or layout changes
- Use a standard audit checklist for each site prior to renewal
- Cross-check machinery, fit-outs, and values with site managers or asset registers

Global lens

In 2019, a retail electronics chain in Glasgow, Scotland, suffered separate water damage events at two stores within a 10-day span. Their All Risks policy applied separate deductibles and event limits. The broker had not advised on this exposure. The second claim was declined under the "per occurrence" clause, despite being part of the same weather system. The client paid nearly £300,000 in recovery costs.

CPD reflection

- Do you confirm sublimits and deductibles **per location** in multi-site risks?
- Could your renewal summary or quote documents defend their structure?
- Are you confident each site's assets match its declared values and exposure?

Chapter 17: Fit-out, fit for blame

"A verbal contract isn't worth the paper it's written on."
- Samuel Goldwyn, film producer and business executive

Real-world case

In 2021, a boutique retail tenant in Birmingham, UK suffered water damage from a burst pipe above their leased unit. Their £280,000 custom fit-out was ruined. The landlord's policy covered the structure but made no mention of tenant improvements. The tenant's broker had assumed the landlord would insure the entire space, including fit-outs. The landlord assumed the tenant had taken separate cover. The result: no clear insurable interest, subrogation risk, and a denied claim. Litigation followed. The retailer never reopened.

Ella's story

Ella had sunk everything into the flagship store.

Custom display shelving. Mosaic tilework behind the counter. Scented lighting systems that changed with time of day. The fit-out cost more than the first year's rent, and every piece was hers.

When the pipe burst, it started above the storeroom. A trickle at first. By morning, the entire floor was soaked. The tilework cracked. Shelving swelled. The LED track lighting blinked once and died.

"It's covered," her broker said. "You've got property cover."

"Does it include the fit-out?"

"It should. Worst case, the landlord's policy will."

But that wasn't worst case.

The landlord's insurer denied the claim.
The landlord blamed Ella.

Ella's insurer pointed to the lease: she didn't own the premises. Subrogation rights were triggered, but no waiver was in place.

The policies bounced the claim back and forth.

Eventually, everyone agreed the fit-out was real. But no one agreed who had insured it, or should have.

"We insured the building, not her fixtures," the landlord said.

"She didn't list the improvements," the broker admitted. "They were new."

"There's no waiver of subrogation," the insurer added. "We'll recover from the landlord."

"It was a pipe in *your* wall," Ella said. "But I'm the one sinking."

The shop never reopened. Ella took a payout well below cost after legal mediation. Her brand, built over three years, closed with a clearance sale.

Mentor reflection

Fit-outs often fall through the cracks, insured by no one, assumed by everyone.

Retailers, hospitality venues, and office tenants frequently invest hundreds of thousands into improvements. But unless those values are declared, listed, and structured correctly, they may not be insured at all.

Worse, when a claim occurs, multiple parties may point fingers, especially if waivers of subrogation weren't arranged between landlord and tenant insurers.

Brokers must actively ask:

- Who owns the improvements?
- Who has the insurable interest?
- And what does the lease say about obligations?

What if Ella's broker had reviewed the lease and itemised the improvements?
What if the landlord's insurer had waived subrogation in writing?
What if all parties had clarity before the pipe burst?

Broker's checklist - fit-outs, leases, and subrogation

- Confirm who owns the fit-out (tenant, landlord, or shared)
- Ensure declared values include all fixed tenant improvements
- Review the lease for fit-out clauses, responsibility, and insurance obligations
- Arrange waivers of subrogation where possible between landlord and tenant insurers
- Use ISR or All Risks extensions for "Improvements and Betterments" where applicable
- Maintain a fit-out schedule, ideally signed by tenant and broker annually

Global lens

In 2022, a café tenant in Christchurch, New Zealand lost over NZ$400,000 in improvements after an upstairs flood. The landlord's policy covered structural works only. The café's broker hadn't listed the fit-out under the ISR. The insurer denied the claim, citing lack of declared interest. The business never recovered.

CPD reflection

- Are you confirming fit-out values and ownership with every lease client?
- Do you have a protocol for structuring subrogation and waivers with landlords?
- Could you prove insurable interest for improvements if challenged at claim time?

Masterclass

Explore this further in my module on co-tenancy exposures and fit-out schedules, including annotated lease reviews, sample ISR tenant schedules, and risk disclosure templates—inside the Risk Advisor Academy Property & BI Masterclass.

Chapter 18: The layered policy that didn't hold

"An agreement is only as good as the clarity of its terms and the willingness of the parties to stand by them."
- Warren Buffett

Real-world case

In 2021, a luxury hotel group in Boston suffered $12.4 million in property damage following a transformer explosion and fire. The loss triggered a layered policy: $5M primary, $10M first excess, and $10M second excess. The primary and second excess layers responded. The first excess insurer, however, declined, citing unproven exhaustion and ambiguous follow-form language. This gap delayed final payment by 18 months, derailed a new property development, and triggered a shareholder lawsuit. The broker's role was scrutinized for failing to verify exhaustion language and claims alignment across layers.

Kendra's story

The fire was sudden, but the fallout was slow.
That's what haunted Kendra the most.

The morning it happened, she was in the rooftop conference room, finalizing design mockups for their next luxury site, an ocean-view retreat set to redefine eco-hospitality. It was her baby.

Then came the flicker. A low hum. Then boom.
The building shuddered. Alarms wailed. Smoke filled the stairwells. By the time she got outside, three floors were drenched, the marble lobby ruined, and the main elevator shaft flooded.

Still, she wasn't afraid. She had insurance. Layers of it.

Their broker had shown her the chart, three carriers, three limits, total protection. It looked clean. Linear. Reassuring.

But the fire hadn't just burned drywall.
It exposed the fine print no one had tested.

"The first excess layer is denying attachment," the adjuster told her.

"They're after exhaustion proof. They don't accept the primary's payment method."

"What about the second excess?"

"They won't attach until the first does."

Weeks turned to months. Investor calls soured. Internal emails were flagged in discovery. Kendra started sleeping in the guest suite she used to stage for media influencers. The master bedroom overlooked scaffolding and smoke stains.

The biggest insult? The gap wasn't even about coverage.
It was about *how* the layers talked to each other or didn't.

"This wasn't a fire," she later told her board. "This was a cascade failure of assumptions."

Mentor reflection

Layered policies seem clean in theory, stacked limits, tidy towers. But in a claim, it's the wording between layers that decides whether a client sinks or floats.

Follow-form isn't always full follow-form.
Attachment language matters.
Exhaustion isn't a given. It must be proven, documented, and accepted.

Brokers who don't verify interlayer wording or walk clients through exhaustion procedures leave multi-million-dollar holes wrapped in a false sense of security.

What if Kendra's broker had flagged the partial follow-form endorsements?
What if they had built a "claims cascade" checklist for each layer?
What if the client had known what proof would be required *before* the fire?

Broker's checklist – layered placements and exhaustion traps

- Confirm **exact attachment language** in each excess layer
- Verify whether each layer is *true follow-form* or contains overrides
- Document exhaustion requirements in writing, before placement
- Build a "tower activation guide" for clients to use in loss
- Flag any "claims-made" or "occurrence" condition conflicts across layers
- Consider using the same insurer across layers where possible to reduce interpretation risk

Global lens

In 2020, a Southeast Asian hotel chain faced a similar crisis after a typhoon loss in Manila. The $22M tower included four layers. The third layer declined due to inadequate exhaustion confirmation. Payment delays lasted nearly two years. The business lost a major development contract in Dubai, and its IPO was shelved.

CPD reflection

- Are your excess placements truly follow-form, or just marketed that way?
- Could your client activate each layer in a crisis, without your help?
- Do you maintain exhaustion templates or "cascade protocols" for your key towers?

Masterclass

Explore this deeper in my module on layered placements and follow-form failure points, where we break down real endorsement language, exhaustion dispute cases, and tower coordination tools, inside the Risk Advisor Academy Property & BI Masterclass.

Chapter 19: The audit trap

"Errors of omission are harder to see—but they hurt just the same."
- Daniel Kahneman

Real-world case

In 2019, a premium coffee roaster in Wellington, New Zealand suffered a fire that halted production and shut its flagship café for five months. The business was insured under a declaration-linked gross profit basis, declaring $2.2 million in revenue. Their actual earnings for the period, however, were closer to $3.1 million. The policy included a 133% uplift clause, but it was insufficient to cover the full Business Interruption loss. A post-loss audit revealed under-declaration, and the insurer applied average. The final payout was reduced by nearly $400,000. The client's expansion into Christchurch was shelved.

Daniel's story

Daniel had always prided himself on knowing the numbers.

The beans, the margins, the blend performance across stores—he lived and breathed them. But this... this was different.

The fire had started in a roaster unit, faulty wiring. No one was hurt, but the loss was significant: weeks of downtime, spoiled stock, cancelled supply contracts. His broker reassured him.

"You're on declaration-linked BI. That's the gold standard. Less risk of underinsurance."

Daniel nodded. That's what he remembered too. But when the adjuster sent the figures, his stomach turned.

"We're only covered for $2.9 million in BI?" he asked.

"That's your declared amount with uplift," came the reply.

"But our actual turnover's over three mil. What about growth? What about Q4 projections?"

"The insurer only uplifts to 133% of your declared figure. You declared $2.2M."

"We've outgrown that! I told the broker we were expanding."

"The numbers on the form don't lie."

His broker later admitted the form hadn't been updated in two years. The client had mentioned growth, but casually. There was no documented rationale for adjusting the declared value upward.

Daniel received just over 85% of what he expected. The remaining gap came from average being applied.

"It was a declaration-linked policy," he said. "But we forgot to declare reality."

Mentor reflection

Declaration-linked gross profit coverage can reduce the risk of underinsurance, but only if declarations are **accurate and current**.

Too often, brokers treat these forms as routine. Clients fill in rough estimates. No review. No context. No forecasting.

When a loss occurs, insurers conduct a post-loss audit. If declared values are too low, even with uplift, **average applies**, and the payout shrinks.

What if Daniel's broker had asked for projected turnover and audited growth? What if the declared amount included seasonal variation or new contracts? What if the client had understood that "declared" isn't just a number, it's a commitment?

Broker's checklist – declaration-linked BI policies

- Explain the declaration process as a **risk forecast**, not a formality
- Review historic turnover, future projections, and seasonal variance
- Include growth trends and recent expansion plans in your calculations
- Confirm whether uplift (e.g. 133%) is sufficient for expected fluctuation
- Document rationale for each declared figure in your placement file
- Revisit declarations annually, especially in fast-growth businesses

Global lens

In 2022, a chain of artisan bakeries in Manchester, UK declared £2 million in gross profit under a declaration-linked BI cover. A fire loss prompted an audit, revealing actual turnover of £3.2 million. Even with 133% uplift, underinsurance applied. The final payout was reduced by over £600,000 due to average. The business consolidated three locations as a result.

CPD reflection

- Do your clients understand how their BI declaration impacts future claims?
- Are you reviewing business growth projections before setting declared values?
- Could your documentation defend the adequacy of declared turnover in an audit?

Masterclass

Explore this deeper in my module on gross profit declaration strategy and audit survival, which includes template guides, uplift modeling tools, and sample audit responses—inside the Risk Advisor Academy Property & BI Masterclass.

Chapter 20: The clause that took back the cheque

> *"It's not what you don't know that gets you into trouble. It's what you know for sure that just ain't so."*
> - Mark Twain

Real-world case

In 2021, a high-end interior design firm in New York City suffered significant water damage after a rooftop HVAC failure during a winter storm. The damage impacted both their studio and client design boards, resulting in an $850,000 combined property and Business Interruption claim. The broker had secured $250,000 in Claims Preparation Costs (CPC) cover. However, the wording limited recoverable expenses to external consultant fees only. The client's use of internal staff time, legal reviews, and temporary relocation planning was deemed out of scope. Only $84,000 was reimbursed. The firm's cash flow suffered, and two key staff departed during the recovery period.

Claire's story

Claire didn't need a full incident debrief. She'd lived it.

The HVAC unit froze, then thawed explosively. Ceilings collapsed, water poured into mood boards, finish samples, staging furniture. Her office looked like a flooded film set—modern chaos soaked in plaster and mahogany.

The claim began immediately. She pulled in a forensic accountant. Her assistant tracked every invoice. Legal counsel reviewed delays on four project contracts. Her own time became an unpaid second job, documenting, coordinating, and managing the aftermath.

"Good news," her broker emailed. "You've got $250K for Claims Preparation."

"Fantastic," she replied. "We've already spent about $90K. More coming."

Then the decline came in, clean, technical, final.

"Policy only allows reimbursement for third-party, arms-length professional fees incurred solely for the preparation of the claim," the insurer noted.

Her lawyer? Disqualified.
Her assistant? Internal employee.
Her hours? Not recognized.
Relocation costs? Not tied to prep.

Only the forensic accountant's invoice qualified.

"We assumed Claims Prep meant what it sounded like," Claire said later. "They gave me a cheque and took most of it back with fine print."

Mentor reflection

Claims Preparation Costs (CPC) clauses vary widely between insurers, and they're **often misunderstood**.

Some policies offer generous definitions, covering internal time, legal input, relocation efforts, and pre-emptive documentation. Others are **narrow and strict**, covering only specific third-party professionals hired exclusively to prepare the claim.

Brokers who assume "we've got $250K in CPC" without reading the clause may leave clients dangerously underprepared.

What if Claire's broker had reviewed the wording with her before the claim?
What if her team knew what time was billable and what wasn't?
What if the budget for claim support had matched the actual operational need?

Broker's checklist – claims preparation clauses and traps

- Confirm whether the CPC clause covers **internal costs** or only external vendors
- Clarify allowable professionals: accountants, legal counsel, recovery specialists
- Set realistic CPC limits based on claim type and complexity
- Educate clients on what can (and can't) be reimbursed
- Provide claim documentation guides to clients before any loss occurs
- Consider increasing CPC limits in large or complex accounts with low thresholds

Global lens

In 2020, a boutique winery in Victoria, Australia, incurred over $160,000 in internal staff and contractor costs following a storm and mould contamination claim. Their ISR wording limited CPC to "external consultants for claim quantification." The insurer reimbursed only $32,000. The remainder had to be absorbed or written off.

CPD reflection

Do you know the difference between generous and restrictive CPC wordings?

- Have you ever explained the CPC clause in plain language to your clients?

- Are your clients logging their time and costs correctly during a claim?

Masterclass

Explore this deeper in my module on claims preparation clauses and recovery structuring, where we review side-by-side CPC wording comparisons, walkthrough client support frameworks, and offer tools for pre-loss planning, inside the Risk Advisor Academy Property & BI Masterclass.

Chapter 21: The contract that cancelled the cover

"The big print giveth, and the fine print taketh away."
- Fulton J. Sheen

Real-world case

In 2022, a UK-based commercial cleaning company entered a national contract with a logistics conglomerate. The agreement required £10 million in public liability, inclusion of the principal as an additional insured, and no exclusion for work near automated systems. Weeks later, a cleaner tripped a motion sensor near a conveyor belt, shutting down a depot and triggering a contractual claim. The insurer denied liability due to exclusions not overridden and no additional insured endorsement in place. The logistics company terminated the contract and passed recovery costs to the cleaner's firm. Their broker was sued for £580,000 in losses.

Tom's story

Tom read contracts the way most tradesmen did: skip to the deliverables, skim the indemnity, sign and move.

His firm had grown fast, sixteen vans, sixty staff, nationwide coverage. Their new logistics contract was a leap forward. He'd bought pastries the day they signed it, still warm in the bag when he tossed them into the crew room.

"Biggest client we've ever landed," he told the team. "If we get this right, we scale."

They didn't get it right.

Two weeks in, a junior cleaner working the late shift clipped a motion sensor. The conveyor stopped. Red lights. An emergency lock triggered across two dozen loading bays.

The depot fell behind for twelve hours. Contracts rippled. Compensation followed.

Tom expected the insurer to cover it. After all, they'd been insured for years. Same broker, decent premium, no major claims. He even remembered asking at the last renewal:

"This should be enough for most client contracts, yeah?"

"Plenty of cover," came the reply.

Only now, the devil came with an asterisk.

"The policy excludes automated systems. You didn't request an override."

"What about the additional insured clause? That was in the contract."

"We didn't have that on file."

"But the contract said..."

"You didn't tell us you signed one."

Tom stared at the letter from legal. Breach of contractual obligation. Indemnity demand. Coverage denial.

He saw the job site less and less after that. Let the crew leads handle it. He wasn't avoiding them, just didn't know what to say.

"We lost the contract," he said weeks later. "But really, we lost the moment we assumed the policy matched the paperwork."

Mentor reflection

Insurance and contracts are often seen as separate realms, one commercial, the other legal. But they meet at the policy boundary. And when they clash, **the contract usually wins**.

Clients sign agreements every day that impose insurance conditions:

- Specific limits
- Types of cover
- Exclusion overrides
- Third-party protections
- Additional insureds

If brokers don't ask, and clients don't tell, **those contracts can cancel the cover**.

What if Tom's broker had asked to see every major contract?
What if the service terms had been cross-matched with the policy wording?
What if the policy had been custom-built to reflect not just the business, but its obligations?

Broker's checklist – managing insurance in contractual environments

- Ask clients directly: "Have you signed any new contracts, leases, or agreements this year?"
- Review contracts for insurance clauses: limits, endorsements, exclusions
- Confirm if the contract requires additional insureds, waivers of subrogation, or non-standard cover
- Match the policy wording to contractual requirements, not just operations
- Document all insurance obligations clearly in the placement file
- Educate clients: a contract is **not** automatically covered just because it's signed

Global lens

In 2021, a scaffolding subcontractor in Alberta, Canada agreed to include the principal construction company as an additional insured. The broker failed to request the endorsement. When a fall incident triggered a $1.1M liability claim, the contractor was defended, but the principal was not. The project owner withheld final payment, and the subcontractor entered voluntary liquidation. The broker settled out of court for $300,000.

CPD reflection

- Do you have a structured process for reviewing your clients' commercial contracts?
- Are you confident the policies you place reflect not just operational risks, but **contractual obligations**?
- Would your file notes survive a dispute about who should have done what?

Masterclass

Explore this in more detail in my module on contractual insurance conditions and broker obligations, where we walk through annotated contract clauses, coverage mismatch scenarios, and mitigation frameworks, inside the Risk Advisor Academy Property & BI Masterclass.

Chapter 22: The deductible that cost too much

"Saving a little now can cost a fortune later."
- Henry Ford

Real-world case

In 2020, a food production company in Adelaide, Australia selected a $250,000 deductible on their Industrial Special Risks (ISR) policy to reduce annual premiums. When a fire broke out in a packaging line two years later, the damage totaled $480,000. Because the claim amount hovered just above the deductible and included grey-area costs, the insurer covered only $178,000. The remaining $302,000 was absorbed by the client. The business owner later admitted he never fully understood how the deductible applied, and had assumed it was negotiable post-loss. The company delayed key equipment upgrades and missed an export opportunity due to reduced cash flow.

David's story

David liked to think of himself as financially savvy.

His broker had presented a matrix at renewal, three options, three deductibles, three premium tiers. The $250K deductible saved over $40K in annual premiums. He went with it.

"We're not a high-claim business," he told himself. "Let's take the saving."

The fire was minor, but messy.

A conveyor belt caught, probably from an electrical short. Flames charred two rooms. Smoke damage spread into sealed stock. Cleanup was expensive, but not catastrophic.

The claim was prepared, submitted, and adjusted downward.

"We're only getting $178,000?" David asked.

“Some costs weren’t deemed directly caused by the fire,” the adjuster explained.

“But we lost stock. Had delays. Paid overtime.”

“Still fell within the deductible.”

His jaw tightened. The fire had cost nearly half a million. They’d structured for savings, not stress.

“We gambled,” he said later. “And didn’t realise how much we were risking.”

The business recovered, but not without borrowing. Two major equipment upgrades were deferred. A lucrative overseas client walked due to fulfillment delays.

Mentor reflection

Deductibles can save premium, but they also shape the client's **real recovery capacity**.

Brokers often treat deductibles as a footnote. A column in a pricing table. But for many clients, a high deductible is a **financial stress test** they didn't know they signed up for.

Unless clients are walked through the *total cost of a typical claim*, they may select limits they can't afford to absorb.

What if David's broker had explained how much a $250K deductible *really* meant in practical terms?
What if they'd walked through a sample claim?
What if recovery costs like labour, contamination, and delays had been illustrated pre-loss?

Broker's checklist – deductible structuring

- Provide clients with a **claim impact walkthrough** for each deductible option
- Ask: "Could your business cover this amount tomorrow if needed?"
- Highlight indirect costs that may not erode the deductible (labour, rent, time)
- Consider cash flow cycles, some businesses have no spare liquidity
- Review whether deductible savings justify the exposure
- Use loss scenarios to stress test deductible choices

Global lens

In 2021, a tech co-working hub in Dallas, Texas chose a $100,000 deductible on their property policy. A water pipe burst during a freeze, causing $140,000 in total damage. After exclusions and adjustments, the payout was under $35,000. The deductible absorbed the rest. The business had to secure emergency loans to restore space and retain clients.

CPD reflection

- Do you explain deductibles as financial thresholds, not just price levers?
- Have you ever walked a client through a sample claim against their deductible?
- Are your clients choosing deductibles based on reality or assumptions?

Masterclass

Explore this further in my module on deductibles, retentions, and self-insurance strategies, including stress test templates, deductible impact calculators, and comparison walkthroughs, inside the Risk Advisor Academy Property & BI Masterclass.

Conclusion: The Broker's Quiet Heroism

> *"What we do for ourselves dies with us. What we do for others and the world remains and is immortal." - Albert Pine*

You've just read six stories.

Some ended in loss. Others ended in recovery.
But all of them shared something essential: **they were moments that could have gone either way.**

In the quiet between catastrophe and claim paperwork lies the true test of a broker's work.
Not in the sale. Not in the summary. But in the **structure of the policy**, the **depth of the advice**, and the **understanding of the client's world.**

You've seen the cost of failure:

- A lease never reviewed.
- A glass panel uninsured.
- A flood clause misunderstood.
- A theft exclusion hidden in plain sight.

These weren't abstract mistakes. They were **human failures**. Failures to ask, to guide, to double-check. And they cost people more than money. They cost **dreams, identity, dignity.**

But you've also seen what's possible when it's done right.

A factory rebuilt. A workforce retained.
A client who didn't just recover but grew stronger.

You Are the Variable

Every story in this book hinges on one person.
A broker who asked the right question, or didn't.

Who reviewed the policy, or skimmed it.
Who walked the site, or assumed the details.
That person, in future stories, could be **you**.

You won't always be able to prevent loss.
But you can reduce the devastation that follows.
You can ensure that when the water rises or the fire comes, your client **has a way forward.**

This book has shown you what's at stake.
But what's next?

Final Thoughts

You don't need to be a superhero. You don't need to have all the answers.

But if you stay curious, stay present, and always act with your client's long-term future in mind, **you'll be the reason someone gets to keep going when everything else stops.**

And they may never say thank you.
But you'll know.
And that's enough.

Now go build that kind of legacy.

Ready to take the next step?

By now, you've seen what poor cover can cost, and what a well-structured policy can save.

If you're serious about becoming a broker clients trust with their most complex risks, it's time to go deeper.

The Risk Advisor Academy – Property & BI Masterclass

Build on every lesson from this book with:

- Clause-by-clause training
- Downloadable checklists and calculators
- Real-world case walkthroughs
- CPD-ready tools for AU, NZ, UK, US & Canada
- Exclusive templates, audit tools, and stress-test calculators

Bookmark your access:
www.riskadvisoracademy.com
And join the waitlist: paul@riskadvisoracademy.com

This book shows you what's possible. The Masterclass helps you do it for real.

Appendix 1: Broker's CPD Playbook

Track your development. Challenge your practice. Build your edge.

1. Claiming CE or CPD for This Book

Most professional broker associations, including **NIBA**, **IBANZ**, **CII**, **BIBA**, and **CIAB**, recognize self-directed CPD learning. Reading this book qualifies if it:

- Is relevant to your job function
- Advances your technical understanding
- Involves active learning (reflection, case study review, etc.)

Suggested CPD Hours: 4–6
CPD Category: Technical / Risk Advisory / Claims Management
Logging Format: Self-assessment or reflection workbook (see below)

2. 15-Chapter Reflection Prompt Log

Use this table to guide your CPD note-taking or transfer to a digital CPD log.

Chapter	*Reflection Prompt*
1	What silent risk was overlooked in the warehouse fire, and how would you prevent it for your client?
2	How could misaligned renovation coverage result in claim denial under your own policies?
3	What do you look for in co-tenancy schedules that could signal a risk exposure?
4	How do you approach flood mapping and emergency risk planning with clients?
5	What would you do if a client delayed rebuild and the insurer challenged indemnity period?
6	Can your BI clients accurately model their return-to-revenue timelines?

Chapter	*Reflection Prompt*
7	Where are you most likely to find uninsurable gaps in declared asset schedules?
8	How would you structure policy wording for long-lead equipment?
9	Do your clients understand who insures their distributor or supplier risk?
10	Are your multi-location clients aligned across values, deductibles, and sublimits?
11	Have you reviewed lease obligations in regard to fit-out cover and subrogation?
12	Could your layered placement fail to respond due to exhaustion or timing clauses?
13	How would you validate a client's BI declaration to avoid post-claim penalties?
14	What contractual obligations have you seen that could void or restrict policy cover?
15	Would a declaration-linked policy structure expose your client to audit penalties or reduced payouts?
16	How would you handle a contingent BI claim if no physical damage occurred to the client's own premises?
17	What are the risks of assuming a sublimit will apply in every scenario?
18	Have you ever reviewed how client-set deductibles impact claim payments and policy affordability?
19	Can you explain the difference between Gross Profit (Insurable) and Net Profit to your clients?
20	What red flags in an insurer's exclusion clause might invalidate expected BI cover?
21	How do you manage client expectations around underinsurance and indemnity triggers?
22	What one change would you make to a client's BI program today to avoid a future failure?

3. CPD Self-Assessment Checklist

Use this as a personal inventory or template for audit evidence:

- I completed reading all 22 chapters of *Fire, Flood, Failure*
- I completed the CPD reflection log for each chapter

- I identified at least 3 areas of improvement in my client advisory process
- I reviewed one or more of my client portfolios for relevant exposure gaps
- I downloaded or registered for the companion workbook or Masterclass materials

4. CPD Evidence Log (Fillable Sample)

Date	Learning Activity	Relevance	Time Spent	Outcome
[DD/MM/YY]	Read *Fire, Flood, Failure* (Ch. 1–5)	BI and Property advisory	1.5 hrs	Logged 3 client risks and one portfolio improvement
[DD/MM/YY]	Completed CPD workbook	Technical reflection	2 hrs	Aligned 2 client policies to best practice
[DD/MM/YY]	Reviewed client lease agreements post-Chapter 11	Subrogation, fit-out, landlord risk	1 hr	Engaged client for amendment

Appendix 2: Quick Reference Toolkit

Fast answers. Smarter client conversations. Greater broker confidence.

1. Business Interruption (BI) Calculation Methods Comparison

Method	Description	Key Calculation	Common Risks
Gross Profit – Additions	Adds uninsured working expenses back to net profit	Net Profit + Insured Standing Charges	Under-reporting or missed expenses
Gross Profit – Subtractions	Subtracts uninsured expenses from turnover	Turnover – Uninsured Working Expenses	Misclassified expenses
Declaration-Linked Basis	Requires estimated annual figures (uplifted)	Declared GP × Uplift (e.g., 133%)	Under-declaration, audit penalties

2. Property vs BI vs CBI Coverage Summary

Feature	Property	Business Interruption (BI)	Contingent BI (CBI)
Trigger	Physical loss or damage to insured asset	Interruption to business caused by insured property loss	Interruption due to loss at third-party site (supplier/customer)
Key Limitation	Often excludes indirect costs	Requires material damage and proper sum insured	Must be specifically endorsed and named or broadly defined
Broker Tip	Ensure rebuild values include code upgrades and escalation	Model recovery time accurately, not just repair	Identify key revenue dependencies upstream and downstream

3. Common BI Claim Delay Triggers

- Poorly defined indemnity period

- Missing declarations or outdated figures
- Complex sublimits or incorrect itemisation
- No claims preparation clause or inadequate limit
- Unclear policy wording on lease or fit-out responsibilities
- Lack of supporting documentation or timeline logs
- Confusion between insured and uninsured cost items

4. Client Conversation Prompts (For Use in Annual Reviews)

Use these to uncover exposures:

- "If your supplier or distributor suffered a fire, what happens to your business?"
- "Who owns and insures your fit-out, and is it declared?"
- "Could you cover this deductible out-of-pocket tomorrow if needed?"
- "Has your turnover or staff count changed significantly this year?"
- "Do you have any contracts that require specific insurance conditions?"
- "Would your current BI limit cover you for the next six months of income?"

5. Walkthrough: Business Interruption Gross Profit Calculation

Imagine your client owns a growing mid-tier business. Last year's figures look like this:

- **Turnover**: $3,200,000
- **Closing Stock**: $200,000
- **Opening Stock**: $180,000
- **Uninsured Working Expenses (UWE)**: $800,000

BI Gross Profit Calculation:

Turnover + Closing Stock – Opening Stock – UWE = $3,200,000 + $200,000 – $180,000 –$800,000 = $2,420,000

Now apply a **10% forecasted growth uplift** (trend adjustment):

$2,420,000×1.10 = $2,662,000 Sum Insured

Key Lessons:

- This is **not** taxable net profit.
- Always apply a growth buffer if your client is expanding.
- Align this value with your selected indemnity period.
- Recalculate annually for accuracy.

TIP: Use a BI calculation worksheet and cross-check your sum insured against worst-case downtime.

Understanding Uninsured Working Expenses

Misclassifying expenses is a common cause of underinsurance.

- Usually Insured Expenses: Wages (depending on coverage), Rent and utilities, Outgoings linked to turnover
- Usually Uninsured Expenses (UWE): Purchases, Bad debts, Discounts allowed

Always verify with the insurer or underwriter, classification may vary by policy wording.

6. Red Flags: Optional BI Covers Clients Commonly Miss

Even well-advised clients can overlook key extensions. These aren't automatically included and can critically impact claims outcomes.

Checklist of Commonly Missed Covers:

- **Additional Increase in Cost of Working (AICOW)**
  Covers expenses beyond the norm to keep operating—urgent rentals, supplier premiums, overtime.
- **Claims Preparation Costs**
  Pays for forensic accountants or external adjusters to prepare a claim. Saves time and avoids underpaid settlements.
- **Rent Payable or Receivable**
  Crucial in leased premises. Missing this could leave landlords or tenants severely exposed.
- **Customers and Suppliers Extension**
  A lifeline if a dependent partner suffers a loss and affects your client's income stream.
- **Dual Wording – Wages**
  Retains key staff after the standard wage period expires. Often misunderstood or undervalued.

Good broking means walking through these, not assuming they'll never matter.

Glossary of Terms

A broker's field guide to key commercial property and BI insurance terms.

A

- Actual Loss Sustained (ALS): The actual financial loss incurred by a business due to a covered event, up to the policy limit.
- Additional Increase in Cost of Working (AICOW): An optional extension that covers costs exceeding normal allowances to mitigate the loss, such as expediting shipping, temporary staffing, or renting emergency premises.
- Advance Profits Insurance: Coverage for anticipated profits of a new or expanding business, protecting against delays in commencement due to insured events.
- Average Clause: A policy condition that reduces the claim payout proportionally if the insured property is underinsured.

B

- Basis of Settlement: The method by which an insurer calculates the amount payable for a claim, such as replacement cost or actual cash value.
- Business Interruption Insurance: Coverage that compensates for loss of income and additional expenses when business operations are disrupted due to a covered peril.
- Business Owner's Policy (BOP): A package policy combining property, liability, and business interruption coverages for small to mid-sized businesses.

C

- Co-Insurance Clause: A provision requiring the insured to maintain coverage equal to a specified percentage of the property's value; failure to do so may result in reduced claim payments.
- Contingent Business Interruption: Coverage for loss of income resulting from damage to a supplier's or customer's property, affecting the insured's operations.
- Coverage Limit: The maximum amount an insurer will pay for a covered loss under a policy.

D

- Deductible: The amount the insured must pay out-of-pocket before insurance coverage applies to a loss.
- Declared Value: The value of insured property declared by the policyholder, forming the basis for premium calculation and claim settlements.
- Depreciation: The reduction in value of an asset over time due to wear and tear or obsolescence.

E

- Endorsement: A written amendment to an insurance policy that modifies its terms or coverage.
- Exclusion: Specific conditions or circumstances listed in a policy for which coverage is not provided.
- Extra Expense Coverage: Insurance that covers additional costs incurred to continue operations after a covered loss, beyond normal operating expenses.

F

- First Loss Insurance: Coverage that provides a predetermined amount for a loss, without regard to the total value at risk.
- Flood Insurance: Coverage for damage caused by flooding, often excluded from standard property policies and requiring separate coverage.
- Force Majeure: A contractual clause relieving parties from obligations due to extraordinary events beyond their control, such as natural disasters.

G

- Gross Profit Insurance: A form of business interruption insurance that covers loss of gross profit due to a covered peril.
- Grace Period: The time after a premium due date during which a policy remains in force without penalty.
- General Average: A maritime principle where all parties in a sea venture proportionally share losses resulting from voluntary sacrifices of part of the ship or cargo to save the whole.

H

- Hazard: A condition that increases the likelihood or severity of a loss.
- Hold-Harmless Agreement: A contract in which one party agrees not to hold the other responsible for certain damages or losses.
- Hail Insurance: Coverage specifically for damage caused by hailstorms, often relevant in agricultural contexts.

I

- Indemnity: Compensation for loss or damage; the principle of restoring the insured to their pre-loss financial position.
- Industrial Special Risks (ISR) Insurance: A comprehensive policy covering a wide range of perils for high-value assets, commonly used by medium to large businesses.
- Insurable Interest: A stake in the value of an insured item such that the policyholder would suffer a financial loss if the item were damaged or lost.

J

- Joint Insured: Multiple parties covered under a single insurance policy, each with rights to claim benefits.
- Jurisdiction Clause: A policy provision specifying the legal jurisdiction under which disputes will be resolved.
- Jettison: The act of throwing cargo overboard to lighten a ship in distress, relevant in marine insurance.

K

- Key Person Insurance: Coverage that compensates a business for financial losses resulting from the death or disability of a key employee.
- Knock-for-Knock Agreement: An arrangement where insurers agree to pay for their own policyholders' losses, regardless of fault, to expedite claims processing.
- Known Loss Rule: A principle stating that insurance cannot cover losses that have already occurred or are certain to occur.

L

- Leasehold Interest Insurance: Coverage protecting a tenant's financial interest in a lease agreement, particularly if the lease is terminated due to a covered peril.
- Limit of Liability: The maximum amount an insurer will pay for a covered loss under a policy.

- Loss Adjuster: A professional who assesses insurance claims to determine the extent of the insurer's liability.

M

- Material Damage: Physical damage to property, as opposed to consequential losses like business interruption.
- Mitigation: Actions taken to reduce the severity or likelihood of a loss.
- Moral Hazard: The risk that a party insulated from risk behaves differently than they would if fully exposed to the risk.

N

- Named Perils Policy: An insurance policy that covers only the perils specifically listed in the policy.
- Non-Disclosure: Failure to reveal relevant information to the insurer, which can lead to denial of claims or policy cancellation.
- Notice of Loss: A formal notification to an insurer that a loss has occurred, initiating the claims process.

O

- Occurrence: An event that results in an insured loss.
- Overinsurance: Insuring property for more than its actual value, which can lead to complications in claim settlements.
- Open Policy: A policy that remains in force until canceled, often used in marine insurance to cover multiple shipments.

P

- Peril: A specific risk or cause of loss covered by an insurance policy, such as fire or theft.
- Premium: The amount paid by the insured to the insurer for coverage under an insurance policy.
- Proximate Cause: The primary cause of a loss in a chain of events.

Q

- Quotation: An estimate of the premium for a proposed insurance policy.
- Qualifying Period: A waiting period before certain coverages become effective.
- Quota Share Reinsurance: A reinsurance arrangement where the reinsurer receives a fixed percentage of premiums and losses.

R

- Reinstatement Value: The cost of replacing damaged property with new property of similar kind and quality.
- Retention: The amount of risk retained by an insurer or the insured before reinsurance or insurance coverage applies.
- Risk Management: The process of identifying, assessing, and mitigating risks.

S

- Salvage: The residual value of damaged property.
- Subrogation: The insurer's right to pursue a third party responsible for a loss after compensating the insured.
- Sum Insured: The maximum amount payable under a policy for a covered loss.

T

- Total Insurable Value (TIV): The total value of property, inventory, and income exposures insured under a policy.
- Third-Party Insurance: Coverage that protects against claims made by someone who is not a party to the insurance contract.
- Time Element Coverage: Insurance that covers losses related to the passage of time, such as business interruption.
- Trend Adjustment: A method to reflect growth or decline in a business when calculating Gross Profit for BI. Without it, the declared sum insured may underrepresent the actual exposure, especially for expanding businesses.

U

- Underinsurance: When the sum insured is less than the actual value of the insured property, potentially leading to reduced claim payments.
- Uninsured Working Expenses (UWE): Expenses the business incurs that do not cease during a disruption and are excluded from BI cover unless otherwise agreed, such as purchases, discounts allowed, or bad debts. Misclassifying these can lead to underinsurance.

V

- Vacancy Clause – A provision that limits or excludes coverage if a property remains unoccupied beyond a defined period (typically 30–60 days) without notifying the insurer. Can impact cover for theft, water damage, or malicious acts.

- Valuation Clause – A clause detailing how property is valued for the purpose of claims. Options may include replacement cost, indemnity value (market value), or agreed value.
- Voluntary Excess – An excess amount chosen by the insured to reduce premiums. It is in addition to any compulsory excess and must be paid in the event of a claim.
- Value at Risk (VAR) – The total amount of exposure an insurer could be liable for under a policy. Also used in finance to assess potential losses.
- Vendor's Interest Insurance – Covers the seller's financial interest in a property during a sale process, particularly when the buyer is yet to fully transfer or insure the asset.

W

- Waiting Period – A defined time period after a loss before Business Interruption coverage begins to respond. Common in policies with Delay in Start-Up or Contingent BI extensions.
- Warranty – A strict condition in an insurance policy that must be met; breach may void coverage even if unrelated to the loss.
- Wear and Tear – Gradual deterioration of an item due to ordinary use and aging. Almost always excluded under property policies.
- Without Prejudice – A legal term used in claim negotiations to indicate that statements or offers cannot be used as evidence of liability in court unless both parties agree.
- Workplace Health and Safety (WHS) – Statutory obligations requiring businesses to maintain safe operating environments. Relevant for insurance due to implications for liability and risk rating.

X

- XCU Exclusion – Commonly used in construction and engineering insurance to exclude claims arising from excavation, construction, and underground services unless specifically endorsed.
- X-Date – Slang in broking and underwriting, meaning “expiry date” of a policy, often tracked for remarketing or quoting purposes.

Y

- Year of Account – The underwriting year to which premiums and claims are allocated in Lloyd’s and some reinsurance policies.

- Yield Loss – In agribusiness or industrial output contexts, refers to a shortfall in expected output (harvest, units) which may trigger BI-like claims under niche wordings.

Z

- Zero-Based Budgeting – A budgeting approach where every expense must be justified for each new period. Can impact insurance limits by requiring a detailed breakdown of asset and income values.
- Zone Rating – A pricing mechanism that adjusts premiums based on geographical risk zones (e.g., flood, bushfire, or earthquake zones). Important for ISR and catastrophe underwriting.

Broker's Toolkit

A Practical Appendix for Confident Property & BI Advice

This section turns insight into action. Use it to structure conversations, test coverage adequacy, and guide placement strategy. It's a companion to the stories, designed to make sure you don't end up in one of them.

1. How to Calculate Declared Property Values

Purpose: To determine the realistic replacement cost for buildings, plant, equipment, and tenant improvements, not market value.

Step-by-Step:

1. **Start with a full asset list**: Include all buildings, hardstand, fit-out, plant & machinery, specialist installations.
2. **Ask the client or property manager for**:
    - Most recent valuation (ideally <3 years old)
    - Construction drawings or previous quotes
    - Details of council/building code compliance upgrades since last valuation
3. **Add allowances for**:
    - Demolition and site clearance (10–15% typically)
    - Professional fees (architects, engineers)
    - Cost escalation over rebuild period (industry-standard uplift)
4. **Use a Quantity Surveyor or rebuild calculator** if unavailable.
5. **Set this as the Declared Value** and ensure the **Limit of Liability** reflects full reinstatement + policy uplift (typically 15–20%).

Tip:

CPI alone is not enough. If the valuation is more than 3 years old, you're guessing—not protecting.

2. How to Set a Property Limit of Liability

Limit of Liability is not the same as Declared Value. It must account for:

- Full rebuild cost (Declared Value)

- Uplift allowance (15–20% typical ISR setting)
- Additional benefits (e.g., removal of debris, escalation, inflation protection)

Example:

- Declared Value: $4.5 million
    -
    - 15% uplift: $675,000
- = Limit of Liability: **$5.175 million**

Check that the policy wording doesn't restrict the uplift through wording structure or endorsements.

3. How to Calculate Business Interruption Insurance

This is one of the most misunderstood areas in placement. Use a structured walkthrough with your client and their accountant.

Step-by-Step:

1. **Confirm calculation basis**:
    - Gross Profit (Difference Method)
      (Turnover – Uninsured Working Expenses)
    - OR Net Profit + Insured Standing Charges
      (More common in the US and SME wordings)
2. **Identify insured standing charges**:
    - Rent, salaries, electricity, bank loans, insurance premiums, etc.
3. **Use the last 12 months of trading data**. Adjust for:
    - Seasonality
    - Expansion plans or new locations
    - Contracted revenue
4. **Add a buffer** for growth (typically 10–20%)
5. **Apply this over the indemnity period** (e.g. 12 months, 24 months)

Example:

- Annual turnover: $6M
- Uninsured working expenses: $2M
- Gross Profit: $4M
- Indemnity Period: 12 months
- BI Sum Insured = **$4M + escalation buffer (~10%) = $4.4M**

Tip:
Clients often under-declare BI because they "assume they'll bounce back." Model a worst-case scenario. Then add time.

4. Example Calculations for Both Property and BI

Property Declared Value Calculation

- Rebuild cost (QS estimate): $3.2M
- Demolition: $400K
- Professional fees: $250K
- Code compliance upgrades: $150K
- Declared Value = **$4M**
- Limit of Liability (15% uplift) = **$4.6M**

Business Interruption Calculation

- Turnover: $5M
- Less uninsured working expenses: $1.5M
- Gross Profit: $3.5M
- Indemnity period: 12 months
- BI Sum Insured = **$3.5M + 15% buffer = $4.025M**

5. Client Prompts to Guide Advisory Conversations

Use these prompts to identify gaps, exposures, and hidden clauses:

Property Prompts

- "When was your last formal property valuation?"
- "Have you made any renovations or improvements in the last 12 months?"
- "Are there periods where this property is unoccupied?"
- "Who is responsible for the glass, signage, and fit-out—according to your lease?"

BI Prompts

- "How long would it take to fully recover from a fire?"
- "Who are your top three suppliers? What if they couldn't deliver for 60 days?"
- "Do you have temperature-sensitive stock? What happens if the power goes out?"

- "Is your gross profit based on accounting definitions or insurance wording?"

Systemic Risk Prompts

- "If your systems were down for a week—could you still trade?"
- "Are you using specialist equipment or third-party platforms essential to operations?"

6. Downloadable Templates (Available in Masterclass)

For Later: These tools will be included in the full Property & BI Masterclass package.

Planned templates:

- Business Interruption Calculator (both methods)
- Declared Value Audit Checklist
- Cold Storage and Deterioration Schedule Builder
- Lease Review Risk Checklist
- Contingent BI Dependency Mapping Tool
- Maintenance & Warranty Compliance Logbook
- Occupancy/Vacancy Notice Template
- Claims Preparation Cost Justification Worksheet

About the Author

A hockey enthusiast never far from a rink, **Paul J. McCarrison** would rather be skating, hiking remote trails, or camping under the stars, when he's not head-down in research for his next project (usually surrounded by scribbled notes, underwriting guides, and half-drunk coffee).

After a lifetime in insurance broking for multiple major international firms, across more industries than you can shake a stick at, and for clients ranging from family-run operations to publicly listed global giants, Paul now shares his knowledge with the next generation of brokers. Insurance was the family business, and he proudly follows in his father's footsteps with a deep respect for the craft, the code, and the long game of client protection.

He lives in Sydney, Australia, with his wife, his son, and a monster of a cat who may, in fact, be a sabretooth tiger in disguise.

Paul's flagship course, **The Property & Business Interruption Insurance Broker Masterclass**, launches globally in late 2025 through major online learning platforms. It's built for brokers ready to become indispensable, trusted advisors in an industry where cutting corners can cost millions.

Legal Notices and Disclaimers

This publication is intended for educational and informational purposes only and does not constitute legal, financial, or insurance advice. The contents represent the opinions and experiences of the author and are provided "as is" with no warranties or guarantees of accuracy, completeness, or fitness for a particular purpose.

All characters and scenarios in composite stories are fictionalised. Any resemblance to actual persons, living or dead, or real events is purely coincidental unless specifically referenced. Real-world case examples have been derived from public records or reported cases and are used without breaching commercial or personal confidentiality.

Every effort has been made to ensure accuracy as of the date of publication. However, laws, insurance wordings, and professional standards may change. Readers are encouraged to consult qualified professionals or official regulatory bodies in their jurisdiction before relying on any material contained herein.

The author and publisher disclaim all liability for loss or damages, whether direct or indirect, arising from use or reliance on this content.

This book is provided subject to Amazon's terms and conditions of use and sale, and all purchasers agree to those terms upon acquisition. For more information, visit www.amazon.com.

Author's Statement of Originality

I, Paul J. McCarrison, affirm that the content of this work is original and authored by me.

While modern editorial tools, including assisted research and formatting support, were used in the development and refinement of this book, all storytelling, structural choices, case selection, narrative voice, and final wording were directed, reviewed, and approved by me.

This book reflects my professional knowledge, experience, and judgment. It is intended to educate and inspire insurance professionals through meaningful case-based storytelling and expert insights into commercial property and business interruption coverage.

Any tools used during development served solely to enhance clarity and presentation under my creative control. No part of this book has been plagiarized or ghostwritten.

Signed,
Paul J. McCarrison

Made in the USA
Middletown, DE
05 November 2026

36543438R10068